Meatballs, Mangia & Memories

Meatballs, Mangia & Memories

Rosanna and Elaina Scotto

Foreword by Adriana Trigiani

Copyright © 2023 Scotto Sisters, LLC

All rights reserved. No part of this publication may be reproduced, distributed, or transmitted in any form or by any means, including photocopying, recording, or other electronic or mechanical methods, without the prior written permission of the publisher, except in the case of brief quotations embodied in critical reviews and certain other noncommercial uses permitted by copyright law. For permission requests, write to the publisher, addressed "Attention: Permissions Coordinator," at the address below.

Every effort has been made to identify copyright holders and obtain their permission for the use of copyright material. Notification of any additions or corrections that should be incorporated in future reprints or editions of this book would be greatly appreciated.

Kitchen Ink Publishing
114 John Street, #277
New York, NY 10038

ISBN: 978-1-943016-18-1 (Hardcover)

Library of Congress Cataloging-in-Publication Data in progress

Cover photograph and food photography
by Justin Jagiello (justincolephoto.com) & Hudi Greenberger (hudigreenberger.com)
Food Stylist: Janine Kalesis
Prop Stylist: Penelope Bouklas

Wilsted & Taylor Publishing Services:
Copy editing by Nancy Evans and Melody Lacina
Book and cover design by Nancy Koerner

Printed in the United States of America

First printing 2023

JOIN SCOTTO SISTERS SOCIAL MEDIA FOLLOWERS

facebook.com/scottosisters @scottosisters
facebook.com/frescobyscotto @frescobyscotto

CELEBRATING 30 YEARS OF FRESCO BY SCOTTO

Contents

FOREWORD—*Adriana Trigiani* • xi

PREFACE • xv

The Scotto Sisters • 1

Mama Scotto • 7

Our Family Traditions • 15

The Evolution of Fresco by Scotto • 25

Food Influencers • 39

Scotto Sisters Delivered to Your Front Door • 47

National Tour • 51

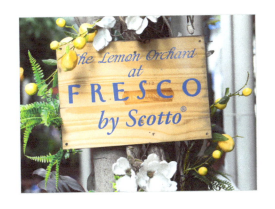

The Wall • 59

Opening Night • 67

CELEBRITY BITES

   Sylvester Stallone • 77

   The Clintons • 81

   Barry Manilow • 84

   Kevin Hart and Chris Rock • 86

   Housewives • 89

Next Generation • 91

OUR FAVORITE SCOTTO FAMILY RECIPES

Appetizers • 97   Soups and Salads • 117

Pasta • 127   Meats • 155

Fish • 177   Sides • 191

Desserts • 199

Cocktails • 211

Sample Menus • 218

Scotto Sisters' Tips • 220

   THE ESSENTIAL PANTRY • 221

   MUST-HAVE UTENSILS • 222

   ACKNOWLEDGMENTS: OUR FRESCO FAMILY • 225

   INDEX • 229

Meatballs, Mangia & Memories

Foreword

The center of Scotto family life is *la tavola*: the table. In *Meatballs, Mangia & Memories*, Rosanna, the eldest sibling, and Elaina, the youngest, have teamed up to share their favorite family recipes, cooking techniques, and a kitchen secret or two that will enhance the way you cook and celebrate your love for Italian cuisine.

Their parents, Marion and Anthony, married in 1957. They brought traditional Italian values to their new family, which grew to include four children: Rosanna, Anthony Jr., John, and Elaina. They also brought their love of Italian cuisine, celebrated with brio in this cookbook.

When the Scotto family gathers for Sunday dinner in Southampton, they bring the bounty of the garden to the table. They feast on vine-ripened tomatoes, zucchini, artichokes, and seasonal fruits and vegetables. The pasta is delicate, the burrata is creamy, and the marinara is hearty. Every bite is fresh. *Fresh* is a Scotto family mantra—so much so that the family restaurant is called Fresco by Scotto. The Scottos take the farm-to-table concept to a new level. Every meal I have enjoyed at Fresco by Scotto is memorable. The experience is a lot like joining the family for a delicious meal at home.

For generations, meals have been prepared, celebrated, and savored in the Scotto kitchen. The legacy endures as the family gathers and makes their late father Anthony's Sunday sauce and pasta, followed by their mother Marion's chicken, roasted to perfection with a stick of sweet butter and fresh herbs. A meal prepared with love is the family treasure. Now you can make those same dishes at home—Scotto style!

The co-authors of this book, Rosanna and Elaina,

bring their Italian-girl flair and moxie to the table. Elaina's love of food extends to her career: she manages the family restaurant. Whip-smart and beautiful (Rosanna says Elaina is also the thinnest), Elaina loves sharing Italian food. Rosanna is a beloved New York institution (Elaina says this does not exclude her from chopping garlic and stuffing mushrooms). You may know Rosanna as an intrepid news reporter or as the award-winning anchor of *Good Day New York*, where she delights in fascinating conversations with everyone from your favorite movie star to the local priest.

When the subject turns to food, Rosanna and Elaina are experts. The sisters were raised in the kitchen. They observed traditional techniques of food preparation at home under the direction of their beautiful mother, beloved aunts, and father. They embraced their grandmother's central culinary philosophy: when it comes to ingredients, go for the best. Rosanna and Elaina are lifelong New Yorkers who know where to find the best Parmesan, fresh bread, or sweet sausage.

The sisters revel in their glorious southern Italian roots and honor the women who came before them. Family history shows that the women in the Scotto family were ahead of their time. They were skilled in the kitchen, and many worked outside the home. However, the family always came first, and meals together were a top priority. Rosanna and Elaina learned work/life balance before it was even a concept.

The preparation of the feast is a family affair. Conversations around *la tavola* are as delicious as the food itself. Within these pages you will find signature Scotto creations as well as confections as old as the bell tower in Naples or the marriage carts in Sicily. Of course, you will find recipes such as Sunday Sauce (page 129) and Grilled Branzino (page 182), but you will also savor inventive dishes such as Shrimp with Watermelon and Tomato Salad (page 124). Desserts from bomboloni to cannoli, served with your choice of espresso or coffee, will leave you full and satisfied.

Marion and Anthony's grandchildren, the new generation, will look back on Sunday dinners just as Elaina and Rosanna have chronicled in these pages. Their memories will become the foundation for the meals they create when they have families of their own.

When Rosanna and Elaina's father passed away on August 21, 2021, his family was bereft, but soon they found solace where he had—in the kitchen, preparing a meal for the people he loved most in the world. The memory of Dad on a Sunday morning, with a dish towel slung over his shoulder as he minced garlic, diced tomatoes, and slowly stirred the sauce, was a comfort. That memory became his legacy. *Stay close. Stay connected. Make this meal, gather together, and think of me.* That is the Italian way. We never lose those we love when we honor the lessons they taught us. Rosanna and Elaina's cookbook is a gift of joy—two sisters, one family, one kitchen, and plenty of love to go around.

Adriana Trigiani
New York City
August 22, 2022

Preface

Thirty years ago, our family opened Fresco by Scotto with a lot of question marks. Coming up on our triple-decade anniversary, it's clear that we figured out the secret ingredient to working in the hospitality industry in New York. Our door is always open, so it's no surprise that we host such an eclectic mix of media, celebrities, politicians, locals, and tourists. An unforgettable night at Fresco is a normal night for us, and that's the way we like it.

Our business has provided us with a lifetime of memories, but what's the point if you can't share them with family? Over the years, we've been fortunate enough to involve most of our family in our business. Whether it's in the kitchen, at the hostess desk, or even outside DJ'ing, our family has been engaged in almost every aspect of the old and new Fresco. We felt that releasing this cookbook-memoir was the perfect way to share all these great memories and recipes with you.

Some of you may remember what Fresco used to be like: gold lighting, rich tablecloths, and an ambience that made you feel as if New York had stopped moving so your dinner would be undisturbed. We were the place to conduct business in Midtown Manhattan. However, staying with that style hurt us in the long run. People wanted excitement and energy, and it took a pandemic for us to realize this. The lockdown gave us a chance to sit back and think about Fresco and to consider how to share even more of our lives with you outside of the kitchen.

The launch of our Scotto Sisters brand came organically during the pandemic lockdown. Like all of you, we were scared about what the future might hold and needed to help our entire family stay emotionally strong.

Our mother and father were cooped up in their Manhattan apartment with no one to visit them. All of us couldn't be together in the city, and nothing positive was coming from the television. So we started going live on Instagram with our own makeshift television show. We would get dressed up, pour ourselves a drink, and speak for thirty minutes about our day. It kept the two of us as well as Mom busy, so that we didn't go crazy waiting for life to change. At first we had just one viewer, but slowly a following started to grow. We became a support system for not only our family but also our entire "sisterhood." The show broke up our lockdowns and gave structure to the "groundhog days" we were experiencing. Everyone who tuned in knew that at 4:30 p.m. it was time to schmooze—thus Scotto Sisters Schmoozing was born. As life opened up and Scotto Sisters was taking off, we knew we had to keep the mojo going. We began to prepare the Scotto Sisters brand for QVC, producing and selling delicious products that have gone on to be nominated on the service. At the same time, Fresco had a complete makeover, becoming a new destination of excitement in sleepy Midtown. We are having a blast with all of these new opportunities, and we want to share them with you.

With all the changes in our lives, people change too. Our brother Anthony relocated to Nashville, Tennessee, to open up his own restaurant with his family. Our other brother, John, remains in New York and has been working for several years in the private aviation business. We couldn't be prouder of our brothers as they go their own way, and we wish them luck in all their endeavors.

These transitions have been difficult without Dad. Though we lost him a little over a year ago, his memory stays strong. He has been a source of encouragement, support, and confidence. He always taught us that when the going gets tough, the tough get going. In his honor we continue the family restaurant and all new and exciting ventures. This book is a tribute to Anthony Scotto and the beautiful family he made. Cheers to you, Dad!

Rosanna Scotto
Elaina Scotto

Dad. PHOTO: Rob Rich

The Scotto Sisters

ROSANNA

I'll begin, as I am the older sister—although our age difference has decreased since I stopped having birthdays a few years back. When Elaina arrived in our family, my life was forever changed. This little interloper moved into my bedroom, where she was always touching my stuff and hanging around. Elaina was shy and introverted, at least compared to the rest of us. She would frequently hide behind our parents, holding onto their arms and legs . . . and yet I thought she was always in the way!

I was often left to babysit Elaina when I would rather have been hanging out with my friends. We shared a bedroom until I was in my twenties. In fact, when I was a reporter on Channel 7, I remember being shamed by my coworkers for still living at home in Brooklyn. Why would I want to move? My mom had dinner waiting for me whenever I returned home from work! And my clothes were always cleaned.

When I began a serious relationship with my now husband, Louis Ruggiero, it was time to move out. We found a beautiful rental in Midtown, where I asked my dad to paint the walls as if I were walking through clouds. Sounds strange, but I loved it. And guess who made herself comfortable? Elaina! On many nights she slept on our couch after going out with friends and continued to do so even after I married "Louis the lawyer," as he is affectionately called.

Louis and I have put down roots in Manhattan, raising our two children, Jenna and Louis Jr. (L.J.), there. Currently Jenna can be found expanding our Fresco brand. L.J. is spreading his wings as the manager of another Manhattan restaurant.

Living "in the city" had always been an enticing

The Scotto Sisters—Rosanna and Elaina.

childhood dream. It was also convenient for working at Fox 5, since I had unconventional hours. And Fresco was five minutes away!

Despite the many wonderful memories made in Manhattan, Brooklyn has my heart. Life seemed simpler back then, with fewer distractions. Family dinnertime was pretty much set in stone. Food was always a reason for gathering, in good times and bad.

One of my favorite memories is of Christmas Eve with the family in our Brooklyn home, with Mom cooking and all the cousins coming over. I swear it snowed every Christmas Eve in Brooklyn. That's how I remember it—just perfect. Once the restaurant opened, we moved our traditional "Night of Seven Fishes" and celebrated not just with our family but with our Fresco customers as well.

Fresco has been a blessing. It's given us both purpose and pleasure. Our children can congregate there, and we have met so many wonderful people. Mom, Elaina, and I have great ideas for the restaurant as we move ahead, and we look forward to sharing them with you. In the meantime, I hope you enjoy some of our delicious recipes and favorite memories.

Elaina and Rosanna.

L.J., Rosanna, Lou, and Jenna.

A Few of My Favorites

Happiness—Being with my family, having a great meal, and drinking lots of tequila!

My favorite meal—Dinner: I love to cook a big bowl of juicy pasta. I make a delicious cavatelli with sausage and broccoli rabe.

My favorite recent memory—The endless brainstorming sessions to reopen Fresco. The restaurant had been closed twice before, and we knew this was our last shot at succeeding with it. During that planning phase, our first phone call every morning was to share ideas we had had before going to sleep, what we dreamed of, and how we were going to make it a reality.

Current state of mind—Trying to enjoy the moment, remembering what we have gone through, but focusing on what is to come.

ELAINA

Rosanna had her own room for a few years, and then I arrived and moved in. Rosanna was mischievous and seemed to take pleasure in tormenting me. I suspect she was not happy I was always around, especially since she was often left to babysit me. Mom relied on Rosanna to watch over me, but little did she know how I was being treated. To Mom and Dad, I was the treasured jewel of the family; to Rosanna, I was a pain in the neck. When I was ten, she and her friends kidnapped me. They thought it would be fun to wake me up at 11 p.m., throw me in the car, and drive out to Woodstock to stay overnight at our family's house. I was shocked since we normally planned and packed prior to going there. I didn't question it because I was shy and knew I had no other choice. Our parents, of course, didn't know about this outing.

As Rosanna grew older, she became the rising star of the family. Her career at Channel 7 was taking off, but we still shared a room. As *she* suddenly became the family jewel, whatever she said she needed, she got. She claimed that her face was swelling because of sleeping next to the radiator, so I had to switch beds with her. I had been sleeping peacefully for the past fifteen years, and now I had to worry about *my* face swelling!

Toward the end of my high school years, Rosanna and I became close. When she began to work in television, I would visit her at the studio. I was so proud of her and all she had accomplished. In college, I became the third wheel to Ro and her husband, Lou. Then they had Jenna, and I babysat once in a while. I did a terrible job! One night when I was alone with Jenna, she would not stop crying. Lou and Rosanna were at a party, and I could not get in touch with them, so I called 911. A trained

Danny, Elaina, Brett, Drake, and Madison. PHOTO: YORGOS FASOULIS

professional had to calm me down because I didn't know who was crying more: me or Jenna.

After college, Rosanna was always the one encouraging me; she helped me get my first job in the fashion industry. I worked in fashion PR for five years prior to working at Fresco. When I married and had Danny and Julia, Rosanna and I were then both moms and shared advice. We have raised our kids with the same values and traditions that our parents raised us with. Rosanna was very supportive of me when I moved on with my life and married my current husband, Brett Yormark. His kids, Drake and Madison, and mine became a blended family. Rosanna and I are so close at this stage of our lives that she, Lou, Mom, and Dad all came with Brett and me on our honeymoon in Capri. Our husbands understand that when you marry one sister, you get the other. We're a package deal.

As a mother, I have taken great pleasure in watching my children grow and working alongside them. Danny currently works at Fresco, and Julia is wrapping up her final year of college. Drake and Madison are both enjoying their college years as well.

Dad's lifelong dream was to go to Ischia, an island off of Naples. But for Mom, it was Capri or bust. We made plans in 2019 and all set out for Capri, without the husbands, so it was double trouble once again. We saw, we ate, we danced, and we enjoyed every moment. One day we rented a boat and went to Ischia, where we found Dad's original home. Unbeknownst to us, the

Danny, Elaina, and Julia.

A Few of My Favorites

Happiness—I'm in a great place right now: my kids are settled, Danny enjoys working with us, and married life and business life are a real treat. Everything is good.

My favorite meal—Dinner: I love to cook pasta with tomatoes (cherry and grape) with diced mozzarella on top.

My favorite recent memory—It's really hard to top the Ischia trip, which was an amazing family adventure with so many fond memories.

Current state of mind—Happy, content, and peaceful.

owner of that house had passed away the night before. When the family living there saw the thirteen of us pull up and mention it was Dad's original family home, they thought we were coming to claim it. Although it was beachfront property, the place didn't have any windows! This trip fulfilled Dad's number-one wish on his bucket list, and we had a great time doing it together as a family.

Rarely a day goes by that Rosanna and I don't see or talk with each other. Our relationship is good because we are not competitive, and our strengths complement each other. Life is a journey, and we want to share ours with you. We hope you enjoy this book!

Although we can't bring the excitement of our restaurant home to you every night, we can give you a taste with a number of our favorite recipes and stories. This book contains some of our greatest hits as well as some new ones.

Many of these recipes are perfect for a family dinner, while others are great for a larger party—we included the serving portions, so you know before you start cooking. We hope these meals and stories will warm your bellies and hearts, as they have ours.

Mama Scotto

Fresco would not exist without Mama Scotto. She is one of a kind, and we are exceptionally lucky to have her. Mama loves being surrounded by her family. If she had her way, all of her children and grandchildren would be beside her.

Let's go back to the beginning. Mom was at home in Brooklyn raising four kids: John, Anthony Jr., and the two of us. She prepared all the meals, hosted Christmas Eve, arranged Sunday Supper, and took care of the house and our dad. It was no easy task, but she made it look effortless. She was a wife, a mother, and a volunteer for the Brooklyn borough president, Howard Golden. Never call her a housewife, because she dislikes that word. She always looks great and would never be seen without lipstick. But don't be fooled by her blonde hair and good looks, because she is driven, pushes us all to do better, and knows what's best for our family.

We have a fondness for our time back in Brooklyn. Life was simpler when we were all under one roof. It was pretty routine. We kids would come home from school, have a snack, do our homework, and then go outside to play. All the while, Mom would be cooking something; our favorite was fried chicken cutlets, also known as Chicken Milanese. Mom had to fry strategically—fry and hide—because if we were in the kitchen, we would each grab a cutlet or two as snacks. And with four kids, Mom would have needed several pounds of cutlets before we even sat down for dinner!

Time went on. John graduated from law school, moved to Los Angeles, and joined a law firm. While in L.A. in the 1980s, he opened a restaurant/nightclub that became the new hotspot. Actors, musicians, models—everyone who was anyone would show up there. John became friendly with Sylvester Stallone,

Elaina, Mama, and Rosanna. PHOTO: ELLEN WOLFF

who later dated John's roommate Cornelia Guest. John is a very outgoing and friendly person, so it wasn't long before he was getting on famously with Rocky. When we got wind of this new relationship, the rest of us were on a plane to California to meet our favorite actor. John recruited brother Anthony to assist him with managing the restaurant. We visited the city with Mom and Dad. Mom did not care for the L.A. nightlife scene and felt that her sons were too far away from home. She loved having everyone together. One day when she was back in Brooklyn, Mom called Anthony and asked what it would take for him to return to New York. His response was simply that he wanted a restaurant. They made plans to open the location in Midtown, but once the financial projections came in, she knew the only answer was to mortgage the house. In that moment, she turned to Anthony and said, "I'm your new partner."

At a time when our mother could have sat back and looked forward to retirement with savings, she took the risk of opening a restaurant in New York City. We are both now at the age our mother was when she opened Fresco, and we can't say we would have taken that gamble. New York City was coming out of an economic recession, and the job market was pretty dismal.

John, Dad, Cornelia Guest, and Sylvester Stallone at a 1980s party in Los Angeles.

The restaurateur who had operated in our space before Fresco wasn't financially successful. When Mom was closing the deal on Fresco, the landlord included him in the meeting. Back in the 1990s, women were fighting to be treated fairly, and this meeting showed how it was still a man's world. The landlord told the restaurateur that if Mom couldn't make the restaurant work, he would give him back the keys. He had failed,

Scott Baio and Elaina.

but he could get a second chance, which wouldn't be the case for Mom. She stood there in shock. She never considered failure. She decided to visit a clairvoyant, who told her that she saw royalty, presidents, and celebrities dining at her restaurant. Mom believed it, and that was that!

Anthony returned to New York, bringing his restaurant experience; we brought the television, news personalities, and the fashion industry; and Mama brought in the politicians. Fresco was born!

In the early days of Fresco, it was really Mom's show, and Dad respected her decisions and enjoyed watching her build the business. Dad was always there to assist, especially if anything mechanical needed repair. But he also loved art and had a great eye for it; he was responsible for obtaining all the amazing artwork in the dining room. To this day, Mama Scotto is the deciding factor in all things Fresco. She has 51 percent ownership and, thankfully, has always had incredible business instincts.

Recalling how it was in the beginning working with her children, Mama says, "We didn't fight. We would argue, and, unlike a fight, after a little time all was good," and it was. We always share our opinions with one another, good or bad. Since we are celebrating thirty years in business, our process has obviously worked.

But we had a steep learning curve when Fresco first opened in November 1993.

From day one, Mama greeted everyone as if they were coming into her own home and never wanted to say no to anyone. This created a problem when taking reservations. At one point, more than fifty people were waiting for a table as she took every reservation without considering the consequences. Learning from that error, we hired a management company to train us how to accept reservations to match tables and timing.

While managing Fresco has changed, Mama's love of food has not. She believes in "feeding the table." She can't be turned away from sending lots of appetizers to some of our longtime customers. She justifies it by saying, "It's for the table," as if the actual table were hungry. (She does the same thing when dining with us.)

Mom is always thinking about the business: how to improve it and reach different markets. It was her idea to partner with QVC in 2003 to sell our food, making it possible for people all over the country to enjoy Fresco's delicious dishes. The venture required traveling to the QVC studios in Philadelphia. Mom and Dad would drive to the city, check into a hotel, and spend hours prepping for a live QVC show. Running a restaurant is challenging; we like to think Mom and Dad enjoyed this time alone

Mom and Hillary Clinton.

Mom. PHOTO: MTC PHOTOGRAPHY

together. This partnership was our first insight for working with QVC, which enabled us to reengage with the service after the pandemic shutdown. Currently, we can film remotely from the restaurant and not have to leave our business.

Speaking of video, if you haven't seen Mama Scotto on Instagram, do yourself a favor and watch. Going live with her during our Scotto Sisters Schmoozing has been so fun. She is unpredictable and politically incorrect, and at times she uses salty language. But she has the right to say what she thinks, and, boy, can she dance! Her cane is just an accessory.

Fresco is home to three generations of Scottos—our children were raised at the restaurant, and we celebrate holidays and everyday meals there. It's fair to say that if you need to find a Scotto, drop in at Fresco. Over these thirty years, we have had the honor of serving generations of families. They come for the delicious food, excellent service, and wonderful experience, but no doubt they return to see Mama Scotto. Almost every day and night, Mom is up front, welcoming everyone. Her big smile and her warmth bring people back.

We know Mom and Dad are proud of the new Fresco. Dad was able to enjoy a few weeks of the Fresco rebirth before he fell ill. He always encouraged us to persevere when times got tough. And while times have been tough without Dad, we know he is watching over us. We are enjoying great success and are excited about the future. We are grateful for our parents, our family's hard work through the years, and the countless people who continue to make Fresco by Scotto their home away from home.

This book is a tribute to Fresco and to Mom. Over the years, Fresco by Scotto has received outstanding reviews in *New York* magazine, *Gourmet* magazine, and *The New York Times*, and has received three stars in *Crain's New York Business*.

As we celebrate thirty years of Fresco by Scotto, we thank our mother, Marion Scotto, for this wonderful life and fabulous family business that she created. Fresco by Scotto is so much more than a restaurant. It's our heart and soul.

Our Family Traditions

Sundays in an Italian household are reserved for two deities: God and Food. Although ours might not be the most religious family, we keep the day holy for our traditional family supper. Everyone is expected to sit down for a four-course meal that will have you praying for a bigger stomach and bigger pants. If you can't make this event, you'd better have a solid excuse, because missing the Sunday meal is worse than any insult. This tradition of Sunday Supper has been passed down through three generations of Scottos. Of course, over the years there have been changes not only to the meal but also to the family.

Mama Scotto grew up on the top floor of a three-story brownstone in Red Hook, a working-class immigrant neighborhood that is now called Carroll Gardens. Each floor of the brownstone was occupied by relatives and had its own unique aroma. As Mom ascended the stairs to her apartment, she would smell Aunt Mary's sauce, with its sweet scent from the raisins, simmering within. But there was no doubt Mom's mother Rose's sauce had the best aroma. She would combine beef with pork for that added magic, a predecessor to Fresco by Scotto's signature Bolognese (page 138).

When Mom was first living in Brooklyn, it was only her and her parents. The cooking was primarily done by our grandmother, except on the weekends. Their home had an open-door policy where all were welcome, especially on Sunday. Everyone in the brownstone would partake in the Italian tradition of a proper supper, devoting the entire day to eating. The townhouse was filled with aunts, uncles, and cousins—lots of them. Mom was an only child, but her cousins were as close as any siblings. It was not uncommon to have more than twenty people for dinner.

Rosanna, Dad, and Elaina making the Sunday Sauce.

Mom grew up in the 1930s and 1940s, when women were doing the cooking, the cleaning, and the taking care of children. On Sunday, all the women prepared the meal in the kitchen, with the little girls assisting as needed, which wasn't much. Mom actually learned how to make her delicious sauce as a teenager, because our grandmother worked all the time in the family chicken market, and Sundays were a day for her to relax. Mom had to learn how to feed her parents and make sure they were taken care of; there was no such thing as Uber Eats back then. Our grandfather Anthony, his brother Joe, and all the other men would sit in the living room with a newspaper, reading it aloud to learn English. They wanted to assimilate into American society but spoke Italian when they didn't want us to know what they were saying. But let there be no mistake: the food was 100 percent Italian.

Dinner and the parade of food kicked off at 3:00 p.m. and would extend past normal dinnertime. The first course was a treat for the eyes, nose, and stomach. A platter stacked with salami, prosciutto, and Parmigiano, served with delicious soft Italian bread, was laid out for all to nibble on. Next came the pasta in the Sunday sauce, which back then was called "gravy." The making of the sauce would start early in the morning, before the sun rose. Depending on your family and the part of Italy

Mom's First Communion.

they were from, this sauce was made differently, but no matter what was in it, it was always delicious. As tradition has it, once the pasta was finished, the sweet and succulent meats of the meal were brought out. In 1915, Mom's family owned and operated a poultry store in Brooklyn, right on Hicks Street. The market had been in operation for some time before she was born, so poultry of some sort was bound to be included in the meal. The grand finale was an assortment of Italian pastries and cheeses. After the meal, the men would adjourn to play gin rummy, and the women would clean. Food would be left out so that when the men had built up more of an appetite, they could make a meatball sandwich on white bread. Our grandfather was not a big drinker, and neither was our grandmother, so they would have some soda pop beside them as they played cards. Some of the younger attendees would drink wine, but that began years later, when we came into the picture.

Sundays in our home in Dyker Heights mirrored our mother's when she was a child. Family galore would walk in the door for the Sunday meal. We'd all go to church at St. Bernadette on 13th Avenue and then head home as fast as possible so that our parents could cook. Once we arrived home, about twenty people would be quick to follow, filling up the home in an instant. The meal began with antipasto and finished

John, Dad, Elaina, Mom, Rosanna, and Anthony Jr.—at home in Brooklyn.

← Our Family Traditions • 17

Jenna, Lou, Rosanna, Dad, Elaina, and Mom. PHOTO: ERIC STRIFFLER

with cheese and dessert. Of course, our generation added our own twist. We would drink Coca-Cola mixed with a splash of red wine. It goes by many names, but we used to call it calachote (pronounced *cal-a-zhot*). Some of our favorite recipes—like Elaina's Tomato Bruschetta (page 105), Mom's Stuffed Mushrooms (page 109), and Prosciutto-Wrapped Asparagus with Parmesan Cheese (page 108)—were added to the antipasto. Unlike our grandparents, we tried to precook as much food as possible so we could enjoy our afternoon with everyone.

As we grew older, the tradition had to be adjusted. Once Mom began volunteering with the borough president of Brooklyn, the work occupied her throughout the week and for most of the weekend, which meant she didn't have time to cook. Luckily, in Brooklyn, we weren't short of Italian restaurants that could accommodate our massive gatherings. After church, we would head to Ponte Vecchio, where, funnily enough, they also made a signature Sunday sauce. Our family would arrive and meet Aunt Elaine and Uncle Vincent there with our cousins. This pivot

Dad making Sunday supper.

in the tradition continued for a while until we started to grow our own families. The Sunday meal is built into the DNA of every Italian, so we made sure to nurture it in our own children.

For the past fifteen years, Sundays have been spent at our collective Southampton house. We three girls share the house, so there isn't a shortage of family to help cook, clean, and celebrate. Keeping with the tradition, our house has an open-door policy for many of our other relatives, as well as close family friends.

Our Sundays start way before anyone else's. In our family home in the Hamptons, at 6 a.m. on the dot, our father, Anthony, begins to prep his Sunday sauce. He's cracking open cans of tomatoes while we all sleep. By 8 a.m., he's simmering the pot of red gold for this week's attempt at perfection. Usually, people wake up to the smell of coffee in the morning, but in our house, it's garlic and onions.

One by one, we come downstairs to start our day. Our father offers a spoonful or a little piece of bread with sauce on it, asking us if we could try some—for seasoning purposes, of course. We're always more than happy to oblige, and equally as happy to give our opinion. Alongside our father, each of us takes a position to complete the smorgasbord we will be presenting.

The eating of this meal begins sharply at 2 p.m. Our kitchen apparently has a tractor beam that draws in everyone, from our kids to our friends, with all of them trying to sneak a taste. To keep them at bay, we leave a meat and cheese antipasto in the living room. That means everyone stays close, but far enough away that they don't interfere in the kitchen. With so many chefs, we don't need any taste testers.

The antipasto is devoured as soon as we set it down.

Elaina and Rosanna with delicious Caprese Salad.

Prosciutto is pulled apart and wrapped around Parmesan, and sometimes turned into a bruschetta on a slice of semolina bread. This is the warmup for our stomachs. Once Dad feels his sauce's six-plus hours of simmering are done, he calls us away from the stove, and we move to the screened-in porch. We always eat Sunday Supper there—it's as integral to the tradition as the food. The setting of the table and the music we play are important to creating the perfect ambience for our meal.

When Dad was having the house built, he made sure that there would be room for the whole family to sit together to eat. Our custom-built farmhouse table is large enough to accommodate twenty people and fills up about half of the screened-in porch. On weekends (when he wasn't cooking), Dad would be out there watching the news on his iPad and smoking a cigar, along with other family members who wanted to relax. It's probably the most comfortable room in the house. If we need to add seats, the rounded ends on the table let us squeeze in as many as possible. Only on rare occasions—Father's Day or birthdays—do we add another table or two. If necessary, we bump the kids outside. Our music choices are a mix of Sinatra and other beloved artists the family can agree on. Sometimes Rosanna breaks out a karaoke machine and passes the mike around. We are hungry waiting for the meal, so we have to do something to keep our minds off our grumbling stomachs.

Once the table is set, everyone files in and takes their seat. The arrangement is always the same. Grandchildren, including our children Jenna, L.J., Danny, and Julia, sit at the far end. Being the first grandchild, Jenna is seated closest to the adults. We and our spouses sit in the middle, and Dad, of course, would be seated at the head of the table, with Mom beside him on his right. Friends are placed beside their host. This unspoken system is understood by everyone in our household.

One by one, with bowls in hand, we then line up in front of the stove to receive our blessing: this Sunday's pasta and sauce. It's like the climax of a movie, when the hero finally receives his reward for all his trials and tribulations. If you've had a bad week, it all washes away with a bite of the Sunday Sauce (page 129).

It's hard not to devour our dish before Dad serves himself. Even if we finish, we all sit at the table until everyone is done. This is the moment when Dad asks how he did, and we all take turns exclaiming, "This is your best sauce yet!" He smiles and says, "Thank you," and we all feel content knowing we are going to have this same conversation next Sunday. Those little things stick with you—the memories that mean the most.

Daddy's girls.

Once everyone has finished the pasta, on comes the main event. Sometimes it's pork chops, meatballs, or sausage. For her famous butter chicken, Mom puts an entire stick of butter (yes, an *entire* stick) underneath the skin and roasts it in the oven. A few of our guests go directly for the chicken, thinking it's the healthier option, but we let them know that looks are deceiving.

By this point, people may consider throwing in the towel, but it's hard to say no. With a few more belt buckle notches to spare, cookies, cannolis, and cakes tempt anyone brave enough to try to eat more. Coffee is served, and Dad has his double espresso macchiato. Everyone moves around to begin the process of digestion. Once coffees are finished, the meal is over, and it feels as if Sunday has come to a close. Everyone feels like crawling into bed.

This tradition has made a powerful impact on our family. Many of our children have written of Sunday Supper for their college essays. The event is meant to bring everyone closer together, which it truly has.

Sadly, though, these Scotto Sundays haven't always gone according to plan. Work, school, and life tend to get in the way. Sometimes we haven't been able to have the meals. With the pandemic, it was impossible for our entire family to come together, but we pushed on. The meals were smaller, but they were still held. As long as Dad was able to make the sauce, there would always be a Sunday Supper.

Looking back, we wonder how we've been able to maintain our weight. If you saw the amount of food on our grocery store receipts every Saturday, you would think we were feeding a professional football team. We eat like it's going out of style. Leftovers would be divided equally and consumed over the next few days.

Times have changed. Dad passed on Saturday, August 21, 2021, and Sunday isn't the same without him. It was truly his day. It's hard to remember a summer Sunday evening when he wasn't seated at the head of the table, smiling, surrounded by our family. It was always a day to share love, and our father dished it out the most. He was such a powerful figure, full of love, support, and patience, that the table feels empty without him. Sundays will forever be our Father's Day, and we will always make him proud by honoring the Scotto Sunday Supper tradition. We raise a glass to his memory, hoping that one day we might be able to make a sauce as good as his. As our father always said, "It's 5 o'clock somewhere." Cheers to you, Dad!

The Evolution of Fresco by Scotto

There's something to be said about dining out in New York City. A special electricity sparks from the heart of the world's financial capital and courses through every kitchen. This excitement can't be felt anywhere else. Nightlife in the Big Apple is always memorable, and the experience of dining at our restaurant, Fresco by Scotto, is unsurpassable. We've become an internationally renowned destination on the island.

What has set Fresco apart? How did we survive for almost thirty years and through a global pandemic to find ourselves doing better than ever? The only way to answer these questions is to take you back to the beginning.

At the start, we flew in from California, left a stable job in fashion, and were working full-time with Fox 5—Fresco was a risky undertaking for our family. We had to devote a lot of our attention to the project, and it took all of us to come together to make it happen. We had little to no restaurant experience, but the stars aligned for us. We hired an amazing chef, who happened to have the last name Scotto, and a fabulous consultant, Stephen Kalt. It was important to us that the restaurant have a classic Italian atmosphere, so Dad contracted with Greg Drasler to create colorful, surreal paintings to hang on the walls throughout the dining room—fifteen paintings in all. One of our favorites is of a suitcase hanging in the bar area.

Our restaurant is located on East 52nd Street between Park and Madison Avenues in Manhattan, near the major arteries of the city, but yet it was a desolate area for dinner. Our location had been used previously by another restaurant that went bankrupt. The area was popular for lunch, but we didn't know if Fresco would draw in large enough crowds for dinner. We took a huge risk in opening at this location.

Our first clientele came with the territory. Midtown is a hub for finance. Suits of the latest fashion graced every nook and cranny of our Italian eatery during the afternoon. At first, people wanted an escape from their offices in the clouds. Soon, our lunch rush consisted of meetings in the dining room and handshake agreements made over bowls of pasta. Word spread throughout the grid of Manhattan, and in every major publication Fresco was deemed *the* host for power lunches.

Where wealth goes, fame and celebrity follow. Once Fresco was established as a prestige location, those lit by the spotlights of Hollywood wanted to share a pizza there later in the evening. Stars like Jennifer Aniston, Leonardo DiCaprio, and Sylvester Stallone were, and still are, regular customers. The paparazzi who lined the sidewalk of 52nd Street never had a slow night—we had to wear sunglasses to make sure we didn't go blind from their flashing lights. As the celebrities showed up, so did the politicians. Our family is all over the political spectrum, but when people walk in our front door we don't discriminate. Everyone is treated as an equal and given the same familial VIP welcome.

Elaina, Anthony Jr., Jennifer Aniston, Mom, and Rosanna. PHOTO: MICHAEL SIMON

The fabulous decor, unmatched service, and delicious food proved Fresco had the perfect recipe for a wonderful night. With the number of famous diners coming in and out of our restaurant, Fresco became synonymous with fine dining in America and was the place to see and be seen.

In 1999 we expanded into an adjoining space and opened Fresco on the Go, with the same tasty food as Fresco by Scotto but in a more casual setting. Known as fast-casual dining, Fresco on the Go was a success, filling the need for those unable to spare time for a sit-down lunch.

You could hardly go through the boroughs without seeing the Scotto name. We were constantly featured on national broadcast shows and even flown out to Los Angeles to present a cooking segment on *The Ellen DeGeneres Show*. We had three sold-out cookbooks, we were on top of our game, and business had never been better! We were sometimes called the first family of Italian food. Those years were such an amazing time for the Scotto family—not only was the business growing, but so were our families. When our children reached a certain age, they were introduced to the hospitality industry. Whether they helped us on the NBC *Today Show*, in the kitchen, or busing tables, they truly made the business a family affair. Anyone involved in a family business knows it's a constant challenge, but it's also incredibly rewarding, and there are lots of laughs. Our lives are so intertwined with the restaurant that it's impossible for our kids to think of a time when the restaurant didn't exist. We were comfortable with that being our life, but times change.

With the revival of the downtown area of Manhattan, a lot of business moved south. A new party scene growing just below Houston Street enticed all the celebrities and politicians. Downtown restaurants were also more convenient for those working on Wall Street. A number of restaurants were given face-lifts to fit modern trends. They looked young and cool, while Fresco looked tired and aged. Though we had done some renovating over the years, Fresco still looked the same. Let's just say we had too many chefs in the kitchen when it came to planning a redesign.

Our restaurant was still a place to meet for those located in Midtown, but we had many empty tables. The lunch rush was slowing, and dinner was quiet. Only our longtime clients seemed to be eating with us. The situation wasn't looking good, and we knew Fresco had to be updated. It took a global pandemic for us to shut our doors (for the time being) and rethink next steps.

We locked up Fresco, leaving all the tables and chairs exactly where they were. We gave away food and told our loyal staff—some of whom had been working with us for most of our twenty-seven operating years—to head home and take care of themselves. We hoped that we would see them again. They are our extended family.

The Scotto family separated and isolated. Scared to death of the virus, our parents holed up in their New York apartment. Rosanna was still working full-time on-air, and Elaina was out in the Hamptons. Our brothers were quarantined with their families in New York. We were all on edge and going stir-crazy, doing nothing after working twelve-hour days in the restaurant. We didn't know if we were ever going to turn the lights on in Fresco again. It was a time of uncertainty in every aspect of our lives.

Launching the Scotto Sisters on Instagram kept the two of us busy and in contact with Mama Scotto. Each afternoon at 4:30 we went live on Instagram for Scotto Sisters Schmoozing, and we connected with so many people experiencing similar isolation. We supported one another, slowly building the Scotto Sisters community. Scotto Sisters Schmoozing continues today, and we no longer have to back each other from a distance. We have hosted a Scotto Sisters lunch at Fresco, and more events are planned. We are thankful for the support of all of our followers.

When pandemic restrictions were lifted, life began to pick up. People were vaccinated, quarantine was no longer required, and travel restrictions loosened up so that people could finally move between states. Restaurants began to offer outdoor dining as a way to promote business. A breath of fresh air was sweeping across the world, saying, "It's time to get back out there." We didn't have to be crazy about walking down the street avoiding people, worrying that we might bring the sickness home. We could live our lives again.

We decided to open Fresco back up with a few extra tables outside. In September 2020, we unlocked our doors. However, the resounding resurgence of dining we desired didn't happen.

In the first couple of weeks, our long-standing patrons came in and ate with us once more, but it wasn't enough.

Live on Instagram with Mom on an iPad.

Rosanna, Dad, Elaina, Mom, and Larry Scott.

Midtown was a ghost town. No one was working in the office; no one was walking on the streets! We were open for three-and-a-half months; some nights we didn't have a single paying customer. Our last day in business was Thanksgiving of 2020. We were so disheartened because many of our lifelong staff had returned to help. We had to tell them once again that they needed to find another place to work. It was a heartbreaking, crushing defeat.

We didn't know what had gone wrong. We had reopened the way we thought was right, but clearly people didn't want to go back to what they knew. Many of our friends had moved their families out of the city, and everyone was happy to be working remotely. How were we going to get people back in Fresco?

Once we started traveling again, the Scotto family made our way down to Florida—all fifteen of us. It was a quick trip, but a much-needed escape from New York. Fresco was still shut, with no plans of reopening. We were tired, but our father, Anthony, kept urging us to reopen. If anyone was the driving force behind the restaurant's new rise, it was our father. He did not stop telling us that we needed to make one more push, a big final stand in New York. If we failed, fine, but we needed to try one more time.

Our Florida vacation soon morphed into market research. We were surprised to find that COVID did not impact dining down south as it did in New York City. The music was loud, and the waiters were dancing with the customers. It was one big party—the roaring '20s all over again! It felt so good to be social as we had in the past. Our large family often eats and wraps up early, but no one wanted to get out of their seats. We realized that this was the new normal. A light bulb went off in our heads: the party needed to be in Midtown. We needed to bring this fun dining experience to our restaurant by reinventing and relaunching Fresco by Scotto.

In our fun and social family, we had no shortage of experts on the party scene to assist with the restaurant's reinvention. The first person we contacted was our cousin Michaelangelo L'Acqua, our family's expert on all things musical. Michaelangelo is a well-known DJ and musician; at the time, he was working with the W Hotel as their head of Global Entertainment. If anyone could get the party started, it was Michaelangelo. We gave our cousin the task of curating music for Fresco and he handed us amazing playlists. A mixture of disco, pop, dance, and rap songs created the vibe we wanted. As we listened, we couldn't keep from dancing and singing along. We're not great singers, but at the volume we play our music, it doesn't matter. We now had the right sound.

Next, we needed to redesign the interior of the restaurant. Fresco's decor had been the same since its opening in 1993, filled with ornate tapestries and a blue carpet with gold stars. We enlisted Lawrence Scott to give Fresco a much-needed face-lift. Larry has been a

Lawrence Scott transforming Fresco and creating the lemon grove in the dining room.

longtime friend of the family; he runs a successful event-planning business and is known for putting on lavish, amazing parties in New York and the Hamptons. If you want an event to be the talk of the town for months to come, you contact Larry. So, we tasked Larry with redesigning Fresco. It needed to be a place to host a nightly party for younger crowds, but still appeal to our longtime clients, all while maintaining Fresco's atmosphere of fine dining.

Our idea for the restaurant's rebirth was to emulate a famous restaurant in Capri. We couldn't leave the States, so why not bring Italy to New York? No passport required. Our request to Larry was, "Turn Fresco into a happy place. Create an outdoor dining area like no other"—reinvent the dining room without losing the classic Italian feel. Larry took the challenge and came back with more ideas. Capri is known for its lemon trees, so he decided to plant a grove . . . Larry's way. In March 2021 construction began on our European oasis.

The decor of Fresco changed into something wholly new. Yellow orbs shrouded in green leaves hang above the tables and chairs throughout the restaurant, and a massive lemon tree grows right in the middle. This aesthetic extends throughout the dining room and in the outdoor structure. Patrons are enclosed in their own Italian garden, secluded from the labyrinth of Manhattan skyscrapers.

We took the seeds of this new look and planted them at Fresco on the Go, which during the day still has the same delicious fast-casual options on the menu. But now after 3 p.m. it transforms into the Sunset Lounge, with a fantastic cabana—a sexy bar and happy-hour lounge in the evenings. Private parties frequently reserve the Sunset Lounge, which offers a secure event space for cocktails, catering, and dancing.

Fresco's transformation took more than three months to complete. In June 2021, we reopened the doors. Most of our old-time employees returned, and we hired a new chef, Ben Kacmarcik, to revamp our menu. We began to prep for our first soft openings to unveil Fresco's Italian lemon grove amid urban New York. Our guests' reactions indicated a bright future.

The music was loud, the decor was vibrant, and a new electricity radiated between Madison and Park Avenues. Diners couldn't sit still in their seats as they listened to Michaelangelo's music. We had trouble turning tables because people wouldn't leave! It was the homecoming we had been dying for, and it didn't seem real. Every night, when our new theme song, "Bella Ciao," comes on, the Scotto team, wearing fedoras and waving white

napkins, dances among the tables. Customers excitedly join in, conga-lining their way outside to dance on the sidewalk for as long as they desire, until the entire restaurant, including the waitstaff, joins in. Nothing stops the nightly party from happening.

Throughout the construction and reopening, we continued doing our Scotto Sisters Schmoozing show and, with each post, tried to capture the excitement of Fresco by Scotto's rebirth. Since we launched Scotto Sisters during the pandemic, we have amassed more than

Jenna leading the "Bella Ciao" dance.
PHOTO: MTC PHOTOGRAPHY

Fresco's new outdoor cabana. PHOTO: ELLEN WOLFF

A celebration parade. PHOTO: MTC PHOTOGRAPHY

twenty thousand followers. Some are longtime patrons, and others are new customers. Instagram has been the best way for us to showcase our ideas about food and dining. We serve an ice cream tower with melted chocolate and feature a birthday parade with sparklers, all set to Stevie Wonder's "Happy Birthday." This dessert parade includes our Tiramisu (page 210), banana pudding, Bomboloni (page 202), and Cheesecake (page 206). The reactions always encourage us to try out new ideas, whatever they may be. We do our best to make each experience unforgettable, and the videos of celebrations we have posted on Instagram have led many customers to come up to us throughout the night asking, "Can we start dancing now?" Our followers even gave us suggestions for the title of this book!

A few months after the relaunch

and with the party going strong, we decided we needed to up the ante. We contacted Michaelangelo once again to enhance our ambience. Thursday through Saturday we now have a lineup of local talent constantly spinning tracks for our customers. In addition, we added a continuous 360-degree video platform for customers to capture, with their phones, their fun night at Fresco. It sounds crazy, but people love this way of creating a memory at Fresco beyond the delicious dishes. Who knows what we will do next?

Fresco by Scotto has come full circle. Power lunches are happening again over steaming dishes of pasta. Our friends from Hollywood are returning, reigniting the sparks and camera flashes. Going back to that painting of the suitcase, its symbolism has many interpretations. It could be a journey, like the rise-fall-rise that Fresco went through, but we like Mom's interpretation the most: leave your baggage behind. When you walk in our door, we want you to leave all your worries and concerns behind and enjoy yourselves in our beautiful restaurant.

Food Influencers

We grew up before smartphones. We did have the first cell phone—the one that came in its own bag. Yes, we thought we were so cool with our big portable phone in a bag! Being able to fit a cell phone in a pocket now is crazy, not to mention all the features.

We started down the path of social media to create something to keep our mother engaged. Initially, our phones had no feature to go live with three people, so Rosanna had to hold up an iPad with our mother on it so she could be part of the conversation. In the beginning, we didn't understand how important social media and Instagram would be in the relaunch of Fresco. We knew we wanted to capture and share the amazing changes to the restaurant and promote all the exciting happenings at Fresco and in our lives. We secured accounts on Instagram for Fresco by Scotto and the Scotto Sisters and we were off.

At first, we had a calamity of errors because of technical issues. Mom is one heck of an entertaining wing woman and a Scotto Sister, too. One day she would be on camera, another day we wouldn't have volume. Sometimes it was just easier to put her on speaker phone rather than worry about getting a live video feed. We leave no woman behind in the Scotto family.

We didn't plan to amass an Instagram following, but during the pandemic lockdown a lot of people like us were stuck at home, and they gravitated toward our show. Week by week we watched the numbers slowly tick up from ten to one thousand live viewers per show. From this amazing reception, we've grown a "sisterhood" of support. However, it took time to find our footing with content creation and incorporating social media into our lives.

Elaina, Mama Scotto, and Rosanna.

Elaina, Mom, and Rosanna.

Our family members at first resisted embarking on the influencer route. They were reluctant to go that direction because the influencer market is quite saturated and not always honest. The influencer realm of Instagram has a negative side. Balancing real life and what Instagram shows is difficult and can lead to undesirable results. We didn't want to show off something we couldn't back up. We have always believed that people came to Fresco for the great service and delicious food, and now the Scotto Sisters had transformed Fresco—still the same tasty food and wonderful service, but with new decor, a dash of music, and dancing to create a fantastic experience. That was the message we wanted to share, and Instagram was the vehicle.

Certain restaurants boast of grand presentations and events. Some places feature dancing waitstaff, while others blast music or present a special dish in a gold briefcase. You can scroll through your Instagram feed daily and find these outlandish spectacles across the United States. Restaurants are trying to capture a new audience because, let's face it, everyone mastered cooking for themselves in the past two years, and they need a reason to leave their homes. Instagram makes it possible for us to showcase our family restaurant to people in Australia from the comfort of our kitchen. Yet with people's short attention spans, posting new content is a job in and of itself.

We had no idea where to begin. We thought that by posting a few recipe videos and going live four days a week, we could create buzz for Fresco by Scotto. That wasn't the case. Sure, we were creating buzz for ourselves, but moving online traffic from the Scotto Sisters account to the Fresco by Scotto account wasn't as easy as it sounds. It's a lot more technical than most people think. A friend recommended that we work with a social media consultant. It seemed ridiculous to think that we needed a professional to show us how to use Instagram. Our children spend most of their time staring at their phones—isn't that enough to call them experts? To our surprise, our consultant Dining with Skyler helped us become professional content creators and get the Fresco by Scotto page "camera-ready."

Dining with Skyler showed us how to set up "thirst traps," as they are called, by emphasizing the gooey, cheesy, mouthwatering aspects of our food. Whether it was steam rising from a plate of pasta or a colorful arrangement of homemade ice cream being drizzled with chocolate sauce, our food could be arranged to be most satisfying on camera. We found that our Eggplant and Zucchini Pie (page 100) is the perfect star of our "thirst trap" efforts, especially when fresh out of the oven. Getting the "money shot" took many tries, but we became amateur food stylists in the process. Photos that showcase the delectability of a meal are truly an art in themselves.

Once we had the Fresco by Scotto page down to a

Mama Scotto with giant golden cannoli.

science run by our editor-in-chief, Jenna, we turned our attention back to our Scotto Sisters page. We had created videos and reels of recipes for our fans to follow along, but they were not receiving the traction we wanted. Instagram algorithms change daily and require staying current with trends. In building a social media community, we needed to put ourselves out there. Effective posts had to be personal, such as posting about last night's exciting celebrity guest dining at Fresco, the Scotto Sisters dancing in the lemon orchard, or a lot of people dancing on the East 52nd Street sidewalk.

In the process of capturing content, we learned that we have a star on our hands: Mama Scotto. Instagram loves our mother. She would always sneak in an "F-bomb" during our live shows, and people needed a good reason to laugh. Every video we posted with Mom became one of our most-viewed reels. It isn't that we had neglected her in the past—Mama Scotto is a Scotto Sister without question—but we had never noticed this trend before. When we did, we began to include her in as many videos as possible where we knew we could capture good content. If we were doing something crazy or ridiculous, Mom would exclaim, "Whatsa matter with us?" Those familial back-and-forths help people identify with our content. Recently we hit the Instagram jackpot with a video featuring Mama Scotto. We didn't think it was going to get so many views, and we didn't know it had until we looked back through our analytics. The video is a simple one, from June 13, 2022, of the three of us dancing in the streets at Fresco by Scotto (look on our Scotto Sisters page for the video with the highest number of views). So far, it is on track to get 3 million views with more than 43,000 likes. Compared to our next-highest video, which has only around 40,000 views, it's ridiculous! We're trying to recreate that recipe, hoping to gain more followers while having as much fun as possible.

With the influx of followers and customers of our Scotto Sisters brand, we have become lifestyle and food influencers. In the beginning, we didn't really understand how valuable it would be to become social media personalities and to involve other personalities with our brand as well.

Speaking with our consultant after both of our pages were in order, we realized that we needed to branch out to some of our colleagues, and we don't mean other restaurateurs. Influencers are the new celebrities nowadays, especially the ones who involve a lot of food in their content. It doesn't matter what type of dish it is. If it's funny and it looks delicious, it's going to get hits. These influencers have created an online world for themselves with their own fan bases and followings that are changing the definition of what it means to be a celebrity. We say this because we saw it happen with our own eyes.

We were lucky enough to have lunch with a few food influencers at Fresco by Scotto. The first were Lil "Mo" Mozzarella (@lilmomozzarella), Cugine (@meals_by_cug), and Nicolas Heller, a.k.a. "New York Nico" (@newyorknico). These guys look like a couple of goombahs who'd be hanging out on the corner by our old house in Brooklyn. Their very old-school dialect is hilarious. Comedy is universal, and so is food: combine the two and you have Nico, Mo, and Cug. Our lunch was enjoyable, since these guys are a riot together. We had a blast serving them, and it seems they had a blast, too, getting up to dance with our servers when we presented them with Fresco's dessert parade. As the hours passed, many young people came up to take a photo with them. We hadn't expected this reaction, to be honest, but with their followings of more than half a million, it made sense. Everyone was excited to see them, just as we would have been to see our favorite bands and celebrities when we were kids. They were all gracious about fans taking photos. Even more extraordinary was seeing the actor Chazz Palminteri, who was sitting a few tables away and getting no recognition. To us, Chazz is an A-List celebrity,

← Food Influencers • 43

Lil Mo, Cugine, Rosanna, and Elaina.

so it seemed crazy that so little foot traffic headed to his table. Chazz even came over to our table to take a photo with Nico, Mo, and Cug!

The influencer Jonathan Cheban, better known as Foodgod, has been a friend of ours for some time. Originally a PR executive, he made his influencer debut on *Keeping Up with the Kardashians*. Not long after that, he exploded into stardom. He began his @Foodgod account and legally changed his name to Foodgod, as well as creating his own food line and judging a few cooking competition shows. He manages an Instagram account with 3.8 million followers. He's a slim guy, so we're always impressed by the photos showing the large amount of food he consumes. We're not sure how he's able to maintain his appearance when he's taking down pizza slices the size of his body. Maybe we'll have to get on the Foodgod diet soon. Despite all the stardom, Jonathan has stayed close to his roots, and whenever he's in town, he comes by Fresco by Scotto.

Foodgod was coming for lunch, and we knew we had to up our game. Jonathan knows what he likes to eat and is always on the lookout for Instagram-worthy foods, whether it's super-cheesy pizza or a decadent ice cream sundae—the more lavish, the better. We treated Foodgod to a classic meal at Fresco. We served our Gorgonzola

Rosanna, Foodgod, and Elaina.

and Zucchini Chips, Grilled Pizza Margherita (page 98), Pasta Bolognese (page 138): all the classic hits. But we surprised him with our massive golden cannoli. He went crazy for it. He took the two-handed dessert and carried it around the restaurant as though it were an offering to God. He finally landed in the bar area, which he determined was the best place to shoot a video. He filmed himself breaking up the cannoli with a golden hammer and then ripping it in half before indulging himself in true Foodgod fashion. The video garnered tens of thousands of views on Instagram, and we are so grateful to him for his love and support of Fresco and the Scotto Sisters.

Each day brings a new opportunity for us to share Fresco by Scotto online, bringing our restaurant a little closer to everyone. Building our Scotto Sisters community online has really made the reinvention and success of Fresco by Scotto a massive accomplishment, and we are so thankful for everyone's love and support. We feel proud to be able to bring our world to you. New ideas for Fresco are being hatched moment by moment, and we can't wait to share them with all of you at home!

Scotto Sisters Delivered to Your Front Door

When launching the new Fresco by Scotto restaurant and the Scotto Sisters brand, we looked to our friend Jill Martin at QVC. Jill's own brands of apparel and accessories have been extremely successful selling on QVC. Her guidance was invaluable. We were introduced to the queen of QVC sales, Adina Miccio. Adina can sell honey to a beehive if she so chooses. She not only is gifted with an immaculate on-air presence but also has become instrumental in the development of our Scotto Sisters line. She has created only the finest products for our brand.

The Scotto Sisters QVC launch was on September 29, 2021—a time when many people were not leaving their homes and dining out. The Scotto Sisters seized the opportunity to deliver Fresco's delicious meals and desserts to homes across the country with the assistance of QVC.

Offering our scrumptious food outside the restaurant and introducing people all over the country to the Scotto Sisters brand was a win-win. Our delicious Meatballs in Sunday Sauce (3 whole pounds!) (pages 161 and 129), Cheese or Spinach Lasagnas, Caramel Mascarpone Italian Cheesecake, and Scotto Sisters 4.5-pound Italian Cream Cake with Pecans are all perfect for a few family dinners or one big party.

In the past, selling on QVC had been a challenge because the QVC studios are in Philadelphia and the shows are live, so when our parents did this they had to spend a weekend in Philly. Running a restaurant is challenging enough, and the QVC shoot schedule was excruciating. You needed to arrive in Philly the night before your segment, which would sometimes air at 4 a.m. At first, we weren't sure if this venture was going to be a success. Thankfully, we no longer needed to drive to

Our QVC queen, Elaina.

Elaina with the Scotto Sisters' delicious Caramel Mascarpone Cheesecake.

Philly—we could go live on Skype right from our home, which has been both a blessing and a curse. On the one hand, it's never been easier to work with QVC; on the other, we had more technical issues than we wanted to deal with. We pushed through, however, and are happy to announce that Scotto Sisters has been nominated on QVC for Best Meatball and Best New Food Brand. Our QVC success is no longer uncertain.

Elaina is the on-air spokesperson, but she isn't an island. Our longtime employee Will Baltodano is the audiovisual technician and even works as a food stylist for all of our products. We Skype live from the restaurant, but it's challenging when the show takes place during the middle of lunch or dinner. One time we were all set up and thought we were ready for the live show. But minutes before going live, the QVC studio could not hear or see Elaina. The studio's plan B was for Elaina to call in on her cell phone.

Depending on the day and time, it's hard to find a quiet corner, but we manage to do it. We truly love our brand and the products we have created for our partnership with QVC. *Buon appetito!*

National Tour

Not many Italian places make food the way we do. We put a unique twist on many old-school dishes that sets Fresco apart from the rest. In the beginning of our restaurateur career, we decided to write our very first cookbook. It was an all-out effort from everyone in the family. We are still using many of those great recipes in the restaurant today, as well as treasured recipes we make for ourselves at home. When *Italian Comfort Food: Intensive Eating from Fresco by Scotto Restaurant* was published in 2005, we kept the book front and center at Fresco. It was a hit, flying off the shelves from its day of publication. It turned out many people were dying to know how we made Fresco so special. One of them was Jeff Zucker.

At the time, Zucker was the executive producer of the *Today Show* on NBC. He worked only a few blocks away, at 30 Rockefeller Plaza. He ate lunch and dinner daily at Fresco and soon became fast friends with our family. One day, Jeff was having lunch and asked Mama Scotto, "Would you want to come on the *Today Show* and demonstrate one of these delicious recipes?"

Mom was ecstatic about the opportunity and, after asking some questions, found out it would be just her going live to do the demonstration. When asked again if she'd go on, Mom said, "Yes, but only if my children are on the screen with me. I won't do it if they are not a part of it."

This conversation led to a multiple-decade family career with NBC and the *Today Show*. From that first appearance, we began to do six to ten shows a year. Our following grew, and the family soon bloomed as on-air chefs. We became New York royalty from our segments on the 8 a.m. hour.

Not only was Rosanna on every bus that rolled along

Rosanna (center) as the Humanitarian Award recipient of the New York City Columbus Day Parade. At right, her husband, Lou, and daughter, Jenna; at left, Elaina and her daughter, Julia.

Mom, John, Al Roker, Anthony Jr., Rosanna, and Elaina at the *Today Show*.

Fox 5 ad with John Roland and Rosanna.

the New York streets for the 10 p.m. hour of Fox 5 News but also the Scottos were on national television as the First Chef Family of America. It didn't matter what time of year NBC wanted us on—we were ready to go whenever they called. Even on holidays, we'd prepare a feast of recipes from our Christmas Eve tradition, the Night of Seven Fishes. To this day we are more than grateful that they keep inviting us on.

When we got comfortable enough, our kids began to join us on-screen. When Mama said she wanted her family up there, she meant all of us, and the *Today Show* was more than okay with having three generations of Scottos live on air. They were such big fans of our family that NBC gave us video cameras for our international vacations, asking us to film what we were eating. They wanted us to showcase the food of the areas we visited and the specialties of each locale.

NBC cameras joined us for two fantastic trips. The first was to Cabo San Lucas, Mexico, at Christmastime in 2007. We spent our days soaking up the sun and lounging on the beach. In between siestas, we went to different restaurants and filmed local chefs creating a lot of seafood dishes. NBC needed us to film an introductory "stinger" video that would play for our on-air segment; if we were going to be doing seafood items, we would need action shots of us catching the fish. NBC was in luck.

⟵ National Tour • 53

Our brother Anthony loves to fish and would always take our sons along with him on these excursions. The fish were plentiful at Cabo San Lucas, so all we had to do was wait for the boys to come back with their haul. We would have ample amounts of fish to show off as being "caught" by us with a little extra "movie magic" to make it real. On the day that we filmed, our nephew Anthony III had caught a beautiful black-and-white angelfish. We wanted it in the shot. We planned on cruising in on a small motorboat and pulling the fish out of the water just as we hit the shore—it was going to be cinematic and perfect. However, eight-year-old Anthony was not giving up his prized fish! We begged and even bribed him to let us use it, but he refused. We Scottos can be pretty hard-headed sometimes, so we knew this wasn't going to end easily. Rosanna began a tug-of-war with Anthony and pulled the fish out of his hands. She ran with the fish to the motorboat, where she dragged it in through the sand and up into the boat. Anthony was furious and had to be held back by L.J. and Danny while we filmed. After the take was finished, we returned the fish to Anthony, but that still didn't make it any better. However, all was forgiven a few days later.

NBC gave us cameras to film our Lake Como family vacation, which was part of a food tour we were doing around Italy, including Rome, and France and Monaco. At Lake Como we strolled around a lakeside town filming different mom-and-pop shops and their amazing foods. We spoke to the chefs in our best Italian, hoping we didn't offend them too much. When in Lake Como, as they say. While we were there, a light bulb went off in Rosanna's head. She had previously interviewed George Clooney, and he had mentioned his villa on the lake. He hadn't said where, but after some research we were able to locate it. It's a beautiful property in the middle of the lake, accessible only by boat. We decided it would be hilarious to record ourselves delivering a pizza to his front door, so we chartered a boat and set sail. Our captain asked us before we started if we knew George. We said, "Yes, of course. He's an old family friend." Our captain had to double-check because of the armed security guards on the island. Of course, we remained adamant that George was like a cousin to us. While on the lake, we forgot about the issue of the guards. It's a beautiful place to visit, and on the water it is even more breathtaking. We were brought back to reality as we approached the island. Not until we saw the armed guards did we fess up and say we didn't know him. The captain immediately turned the boat around. We decided it was best

Mom and Dad at Lake Como, Italy.

waiting for our formal invitation to your beautiful home, and pizza's on us!

Not long after our *Today Show* appearances began, other shows started to call. The Scottos have cooked on *The Tony Danza Show*, *The Rosie O'Donnell Show*, and *The Ellen DeGeneres Show*. Ellen was a longtime customer of ours when she worked in New York and would come to Fresco with her mother. She flew us out twice to be on her show and rolled out the red carpet for the entire Scotto family. We had our own green room and were given a majority of the run time. We were able to sit down and speak with her about family, food, and funny moments. Ellen mentioned how she had so much fun shooting our cookbook with us and surprised us with a photo of her photoshopped onto the cover—you can find it on our wall of fame at Fresco. We were treated

to just eat the pizza with the Scottos back at our resort. As the boat was changing course, we noticed someone stick their head out of a window and then disappear. We believe it was George. So, Mr. Clooney, we're

Mom, Katie Couric, John, Rosanna, Anthony Jr., and Elaina at the *Today Show*.

The book cover altered by Ellen DeGeneres.
Left to right: Elaina, Anthony Jr., John, Rosanna, Ellen, and Mom.

like family on the show, and we are thankful for our time with Ellen.

Rosanna had been working at Fox 5 for more than twenty-five years and was feeling a little left out because, while we were on these various national programs, we had not yet been on her show. Fox 5 had been her work family since 1986, but her biological family was out on every other channel. Rosanna pitched the Scotto family as a segment, and soon we were all cooking together on Fox 5. That relationship continues to this day. The Scotto Sisters have even co-hosted the *Good Day New York* 9 a.m. hour when Rosanna needed a guest host. It's been a blessing to be able to get our family on television and to share the food that has been a cornerstone of our lives.

The Wall

If you've been to our restaurant, you've probably passed a hallway filled with photographs. You could sit there for hours and not even see all of them. The photos on this wall capture the history of Fresco: our friends, our family, all the celebrities who have dined with us, and all the good times we've had.

We started The Wall because we wanted to display the many, many amazing photos we had showing our staff, our appearances on NBC's *Today Show*, and events held at Fresco. The photo area was small at first, covering only the first corner of the wall leading toward the upstairs dining room. The Wall soon grew to cover most of the hallway, where this photo history of the restaurant now dominates the space. Some of the celebrities in the pictures might have come in just for lunch or dinner, while others are longtime regular customers who continue to be seen after the reopening of Fresco as often as they were before.

We have had a long association with the New York Yankees, feeding many Yankee players, like Jorge Posada and Paul O'Neill, as well as the general manager, George Steinbrenner III. George loved Fresco and came in so frequently that we had to make sure his table, the one right at the front of the dining room, was always open for him. In 2006 the Scotto family was invited to take over the Yankee Stadium Clubhouse to prepare some of his favorite dishes. George loved the Fresco staple of Rigatoni with Chicken and Veal Bolognese.

You can find photos of George, both at Fresco and at Yankee Stadium, on The Wall. He loved our food so much that he gave us a spot in the Clubhouse to cater at the stadium. A plaque built right into the main pillar of the restaurant says, "This is where the planning begins." That plaque commemorates the times George would

Elaina, Rosanna, George Steinbrenner, and Mom.

sit with us at the beginning of each season and plan his strategy for the year to come.

In September 2014 the usually private Barbra Streisand chose Fresco for a birthday celebration for her longtime manager, Marty Erlichman. Barbra and her husband, James Brolin, hosted the party in a private dining room. The menu included many of Fresco's classic dishes, including Grilled Pizza Margherita (page 98), Potato and Zucchini Chips, Signature Meatballs (page 161), and Grilled Branzino (page 182).

Regis Philbin was a dear friend and a great customer. On one occasion all of our staff dressed like him in the "Regis look" for a night. Because we supplied uniforms for the staff, back in the day, we showcased Regis's clothing line. Regis and his good friend Don Rickles often dined with their wives at Fresco. We have a photo of Regis with his co-host Kathie Lee Gifford and another of him with co-host Kelly Ripa on The Wall. Regis and Kelly dined frequently in our restaurant throughout the entire time they were on television together.

Rosanna with Regis Philbin.

Rosanna with Barbra Streisand.

Fresco by Scotto staff wearing the Regis Philbin line of clothing.

Elaina, Magic Johnson, and Rosanna.

Elaina, Jay-Z, and Anthony Jr.

Ivana Trump with Rosanna.

Most recently, Magic Johnson enjoyed a great meal at Fresco. Upon exiting, he showed off his best dance moves, causing a frenzy outside.

In January 2019, Jay-Z and Roc Nation executives dined in Fresco's private room, enjoying meatballs, chips, and branzino. A year prior to her death, in July 2021, Ivana Trump dined here with a friend. She was a repeat customer and a good friend of the family.

People like Nick Cannon, Jessica Simpson, Nick Jonas, Paula Abdul, Miranda Lambert, Steve Harvey, and others have all been spotted here. And Mama Scotto would be upset if we didn't mention her affection for Dee Snider of Twisted Sister. The two seem a most unlikely match—however, they got on famously.

In addition, many politicians have sat with us as well. Heavy hitters from both political parties have dined with us at Fresco, including President Biden, President Clinton, and First Lady Clinton. Recently New York City Mayor Eric Adams—a vegan who enjoyed Zucchini Chips and Larry's Lemon Capellini Primavera (page 134)—came for dinner. On his way out of the restaurant, he danced to the song "Native New Yorker," surrounded by fifty native New Yorkers dancing to celebrate his election. President Trump was a customer long before his presidency. He was a big fan of the Fresco Prime Rib (page 156)—Mom would give him a double order to make it look bigger, because he would order it well-done. We even catered to Benjamin Netanyahu, who was here on a diplomatic trip.

The most prominent photos on display are of our family's television appearances. We have a photo of almost

Mom with Dee Snider.

← The Wall • 63

Mom, Rosie, and Anthony Jr. at the *Rosie O'Donnell Show*.

Kristin Chenoweth, Rosanna, and Elaina. PHOTO: MICHAEL SIMON

every time we cooked on national television from 2000 to 2018, especially on the *Today Show*. These photos cover a substantial amount—at least 65 percent—of the hallway. Looking at all these appearances, you might think that our restaurant had been sponsored by NBC. The network has been so generous to feature our family the countless times they did, and we like to consider some of the hosts we worked with as our TV family. Al Roker, Hoda Kotb, and many other hosts we've shared the screen with have also shared a plate with us in the city or out in the Hamptons. Recently the *Today* hosts attended a long-overdue post-pandemic lunch at Fresco. The team had been avoiding group get-togethers outside the studio. We were honored that they chose our family to host their first gathering.

Besides NBC and the *Today Show*, we have been on many other national programs, such as *Bethenny*, *The Steve Harvey Morning Show*, *The Dr. Oz Show*, *The Ellen DeGeneres Show*, and so many others. On *The Rosie O'Donnell Show* we were told that all of us Scottos together were too much. Rosie felt that the whole family would be too overwhelming all on one show, so she separated us. We taped two different shows in one day, first with Mom and Anthony and next with the two of us.

Back row: Theresa Scotto, Elaina Scotto, Danny Faucetta, L.J. Ruggiero, Rosanna Scotto, and Louis Ruggiero.
Middle row: Anthony Scotto Jr., Jenna Ruggiero, Anthony Scotto Sr., Marion Scotto, John Scotto, Maria Elena Scotto, Gabriella Scotto, and Anthony Scotto III.
Front row: Julia Faucetta, Andrew Scotto, and Bianca Scotto.
PHOTO: TINA RUPP

Like the broadcasters on NBC, some of these hosts have also become part of our family, spending time with us off-screen. And let's not forget our actual TV family at Fox 5. Rosanna is the co-host of *Good Day New York*, which has graciously had us on the show for segments and even as co-hosts over the past twenty-nine years. It's always fun to look back on the many bad hairstyles we've all had throughout the years!

Our Hollywood photos are great and make us proud of the work we have done, but the photos of our Fresco family are very important as well. Many photos show our staff during our first Halloween in the restaurant, when they all dressed up in different costumes. We have photos of many of our staff throughout the years as they have come and gone. We make sure to honor them, since this place wouldn't run without them.

Finally, we should mention the photos of our family. A few are high up on the main wall, showing how our family has grown over the years. For the *Family Circle* magazine photo shoot we were dressed in blue and white like the homes along the Mediterranean. Every member of our Scotto family is featured front and center.

The number of photos has now outgrown the wall space. Over the years some photos have had to be retired, but all are safely stored and treasured.

The Wall represents our history through all the good times and bad. We are looking forward to including more photos of our future with the restaurant and all the endeavors that come with it.

Opening Night

The first opening night of Fresco was almost thirty years ago, in November 1993. We were all so nervous because this was our first restaurant. We had no real idea about how to handle the many issues that could arise when serving people. Our entire family went through a major learning curve, but there's no messing with the Scottos when we work together. We were able to overcome every obstacle we faced, and we launched a successful family restaurant serving so much more than delicious food. We created a destination that offered a wonderful experience for all who visited.

We call this our first opening night because our second came in June 2021 with the rebirth of Fresco by Scotto. For more than twenty-seven years the restaurant had remained the same, and we had many older customers who loved everything about Fresco, but we knew the hospitality industry was changing. Fresco needed to be brought into the current era. It had begun to look so tired and old that it was hard to entice a new, younger crowd, one looking for a more high-energy setting. People wanted more than just delicious food—they wanted to get out and dance—so Fresco needed to evolve. As the world stood still during the pandemic shutdown, so did the restaurant; the closing offered us the opportunity to reinvent and transform Fresco. When it was time to unveil the new Fresco by Scotto to the public, the timing was perfect: summer had just begun, and everyone wanted to get out and shake off the negativity of lockdown.

We were excited to show everyone our new concept and were confident that the new Fresco by Scotto would WOW. We had the best team we could ask for, and they had gone above and beyond our initial ideas. Approaching

Rosanna and Elaina on Opening Night. PHOTO: Eric Striffler

PHOTO: Eric Striffler

the restaurant on 52nd Street, guests were excited to see our outdoor lemon grove, decorated arches with hanging vines, lemon trees, and beautiful lighting. The lemon trees carried over into the dining room, highlighting the magnificent paintings our father had commissioned for the restaurant when it first opened in 1993.

The new décor was a wonderful blending of the classic and new Fresco. Benjamin Kacmarcik, Fresco's executive chef, expanded our menu, introducing wonderful new menu items and refreshing Fresco's classic dishes. However, even after running a successful restaurant for twenty-seven years, we were not feeling any more confident than we had on our first opening night.

Tensions were high in the dining room. We felt we were starting from scratch once more. For a split second, it was almost as if we were trying to figure out the locations of each of the tables. Chef Ben was at the helm for the first time as well, and we didn't know if the food would come out fast or come out hot. It was a learning curve for us all. Besides the internal worries, looking outside didn't give us much confidence either. Offices in Midtown were vacant because many people were working from home or functioning in a hybrid work environment. No one was walking down the street—we seemed to be opening in a ghost town. We didn't know if people were going to come back to Midtown to see us. We held our breath.

We made sure to do our due diligence. We invited many of our influential friends from all different media, such as print, screen, and radio, including Rosanna's colleagues from Fox, ABC, NBC, Z100, and CBS. Many of the people whom we invited told us how sad they were that they couldn't dine at Fresco during the pandemic lockdown. We told them, "Fresco is back, better

Dad, Jenna, and Rosanna. PHOTO: Eric Striffler.

than ever, and eagerly waiting to serve you!" We hoped they would stay true to their word and help promote the Fresco relaunch on their platforms. Many of our friends said they would be there for opening night. We made sure to spread them out in the dining room and outside as much as possible. The music playing throughout the restaurant was key to creating the energetic, fun vibes, with songs ranging from Italian covers of pop songs to Barry White.

The Fresco reintroduction into society needed to be seamless. The future of our family's restaurant was riding on a successful relaunch. The Scotto Sisters had taken the reins, and we did not want to disappoint.

We opened the doors on that June night, and everyone invited showed up. We had Kelly Ripa and her husband, Mark Consuelos, Wendy Williams with her own group, and Elvis Duran sandwiched in between. Jill Martin and Rob Shuter were both in attendance. In the dining room, you could find Larry Scott, Lynn Scotti, Dr. Paul Frank, dermatologist to the stars, as well as CBS News Anchor Chris Wragge, and business mogul Steven Starker with his wife, Farrel, all at the same table.

We were so pleased these guests had come for our first night back, but we only wished they had shown up at different times. It's hard to serve food when you have all the tables inside the restaurant and all the tables outside waiting, especially with a new head chef. A lot can go wrong with a pressured kitchen, especially on opening night, but these challenges were no match for our team.

The dishes were coming out hot, fast, and delicious just as they always had. Rounds of drinks were being shuttled in between courses to all the tables. People were holding

Kelly Ripa, Wendy Williams, and Rosanna. PHOTO: MICHAEL SIMON

up cocktails and toasting the new Fresco. Laughter was filling up the dining room and street, almost overpowering the music we had blasting from our speakers. It was clear from our point of view that people were having a great time. We would check in on our friends and they assured us that they were having a blast. The guests stayed for so long that we were having difficulty turning tables! It was a massive block party on 52nd Street. Fresco by Scotto was back with a new look and vibe, and everyone loved it. People were literally dancing in the street.

We didn't let this successful relaunch party assuage our fears. We needed to make sure people were talking about Fresco. We wanted to be current and part of the daily conversation. We didn't breathe a sigh of relief until the next morning.

We woke up to a newsfeed from all over the Internet, television, print, and radio celebrating the new Fresco by Scotto and reporting on how amazing the Fresco reopening had been. Our friends were talking about how fun and fabulous their food and the experience was. On *Live with Kelly and Ryan*, Kelly Ripa raved, "I felt like I was in Italy in a grotto in Capri and the food is always

Elaina, Larry Scott, Mom, and Rosanna.

Kelly Ripa and Rosanna. PHOTO: MICHAEL SIMON

extraordinary." All reports were positive, and audiences were encouraged to make reservations at Fresco immediately to escape the claustrophobic life of lockdown in the middle of Manhattan. Many reported that it felt as if they had traveled out of the United States to an Italian paradise, where you could socialize without feeling as though you were doing something wrong. We made sure everyone was safe, and assured customers they were able to eat and enjoy as they normally had pre-pandemic.

The buzz coursed through the wires, and reservations were pouring in. The next few nights we had Cindy Adams of the *New York Post*, social media influencer Nina Cooper, Hall-of-Fame baseball player Willie Randolph, and even soon-to-be Mayor Eric Adams. The same reopening vibe continued through that second night. People were dancing, singing, drinking, and recording themselves having a great time—the perfect kickoff to summer in New York City. No one was in a rush to leave, and we had the same issue of not turning tables. The food was delicious, and the party had just begun.

Chef Ben did an amazing job bringing a new flair to our menu. We served our new dip assortment and Larry's Lemon Capellini Primavera (page 134), which is our ode to our party planner extraordinaire Larry Scott's breathtaking work. People were raving about the new recipes, and even said that some of our old dishes were tastier than before. We were ecstatic that people were so happy with our changes. Everything had fallen into place perfectly, and we were filling up our reservation books from that moment on, but the buzz didn't stop there.

After that first week of openings, the praise continued. Kelly Ripa on *Live with Kelly and Ryan* kept mentioning her dinner on opening night for about two weeks or so. It's uncommon to be mentioned so often on television, so that was truly a blessing. On social media, we were blowing up as the new hot spot in Midtown Manhattan. Photos of Fresco's food, VIPs, and videos of people dancing were trending. Elvis Duran from Z100 could not stop mentioning what a time it had been eating at Fresco. But the real defining moment of our success was when Jaret Keller, owner of Key Group, our amazing public relations company, called and said, "Be ready. *The New York Times* is coming over at 4 p.m. to photograph." We needed to be certain they captured the new and improved Fresco, so we made sure to get a group dancing on the sidewalk. The article was our final validation. Clearly, we had been right from our initial invitations: Fresco by Scotto was back and better than ever!

Page Six

Barbra Streisand throws bash for longtime manager

Barbra Streisand threw a birthday bash for her manager Marty Erlichman, who's repped her since 1961, at Fresco by Scotto on Friday. Streisand hosted the grand feast in a private room with hubby James Brolin.

"Barbra planned the entire evening, and even made sure Marty's favorite foods were on the menu," a spy said. "The decor was all white with lots of white candles."

Guests included Ron Delsener and Michael Cohl.

Busy Streisand earlier taped a rare appearance on "The Tonight Show" to air Monday.

Erlichman once recalled in Vanity Fair of discovering Babs: "Out walked this 18-year-old singer as [an] opening act. She sang five songs ... I had chills through all of them."

Page Six

Israeli Prime Minister Benjamin Netanyahu lunches in NYC

After addressing of the threat of Hamas and ISIS in a speech at the UN General Assembly on Monday, Israeli Prime Minister Benjamin Netanyahu headed for lunch in Midtown at Fresco by Scotto — with a small army of 30 security guards.

Spies tell us that Bibi arrived at the small lunch hosted by Las Vegas casino billionaire Sheldon Adelson for five people, for which "every single customer at the restaurant had to go through a metal detector," as the leader was flanked by Israeli and American guards.

"The entire block was closed," the spy said, adding, "There were even Secret Service men on the roof."

We hear that Netanyahu opted for a veal chop as he held court.

Page Six

Hart Rock Cafe

CHRIS Rock and Kevin Hart closed down Midtown hot spot Fresco by Scotto, spies tell Page Six. The duo's in town for their comedy tour and are working on a documentary. They arrived at the eatery with a "crew of 13 and a bunch of security," a spy said. The group ordered an Italian feast including veal chops, mashed potatoes and sauteed spinach, plus cocktails made with Hart's Gran Coramino tequila. A spy exclusively said, "At first, it looked like they were having a very serious conversation about their lives and careers. Then, they started to laugh about going to a variety of smaller comedy clubs around the city to surprise audiences."

Page Six

Stars are back at Fresco by Scotto after it was shuttered by COVID

Elaina and Rosanna Scotto at the 19th Food Network South Beach Wine and Food Festival in 2020

After being shuttered by the pandemic, Fresco By Scotto is back to its star-studded self.

Back in December, "Good Day New York" host Rosanna Scotto, whose family owns the 52nd Street power-dining spot, told us it was being "put on pause."

"We tried our best, but Midtown is empty. We hope when people come back to work, we can reopen," she added at the time.

The family also posted on social media, "We are filled with so much emotion ... 27 years of meeting so many wonderful people at our restaurant," The heartfelt message also thanked the "incredible staff"

But the 28-year-old restaurant — which has undergone a major redesign to add more outdoor space — opened its doors once again this week.

The restaurant had a friends-and-family opening on Tuesday, Wednesday and Thursday and it'll be open to the public starting on the 15th.

Page Six

Holy cannoli!

THE star of "Tulsa King" got the royal treatment in Manhattan this week. Sylvester Stallone — who's been spotted filming the upcoming Paramount+ series around town — dined at power spot Fresco by Scotto on Wednesday, we hear, and the eatery pulled out all the stops for the star. A source told Page Six that Stallone was dining with a group of 10 people, including his daughters Sistine, 23, and Sophia, 25, plus a production crew of a reality show that the younger Stallones are filming with their sister, Scarlet, 19. Said a spy: "Sly ate a large plate of rigatoni Bolognese with a giant meatball on top." Fit for a boxer! Then, "at the end of their meal, the restaurant blasted the 'Rocky' theme song and the staff brought out a giant golden cannoli." Co-owner and "Good Day New York" host Rosanna Scotto's daughter, Jenna, "carried a sign that read 'Welcome Sly!'" Stallone is known as a regular at the power haunt. In "Tulsa King," his first-ever TV show, he plays a mob boss who's released from prison after 25 years and exiled to Tulsa, Okla. The series is from "Yellowstone" creator Taylor Sheridan.

CELEBRITY BITES

Sylvester Stallone

Over the years we have gotten to know Sylvester, or Sly as we call him. We first made the connection back in the 1980s in Los Angeles. Since those days in California, our family's relationship with Sylvester has grown. We've introduced our kids to him whenever we had the chance, and he's brought his own daughters, Sophia, Sistine, and Scarlet, and his wife, Jennifer, into Fresco for dinner. There was a bit of time when Sly wasn't coming around a lot, either staying in L.A. or heading downtown, yet we still remained in touch.

In August 2021, we were having a mourning dinner for our dad up in the private room of Fresco. It was an intimate gathering of only family and Dad's closest friends. It was quiet at first, but once the drinks started around, the vibe lightened up. During dessert, John received a phone call from none other than Sylvester. John spoke to him briefly and then ran over to Mom and handed her the phone. Sylvester shared his condolences and talked about how much of a "stand-up guy" our father was. It meant the world to us.

Sly recently made an appearance at Fresco with two of his daughters, Sistine and Sophia, along with a crew for his reality show. The six of them sat in our new outdoor dining structure under the green vines. They ordered drinks, shot a couple of takes, and were enjoying themselves before the first plates of food arrived. The Stallones, especially Sly, are very conscientious eaters; he has to maintain a certain physique for his roles. Vegetables and lean meats were ordered for everyone to enjoy, but for his entrée, Sly ordered Fresco's famous Pasta Bolognese (page 138). He placed one of our signature meatballs right on top of the dish—a meal suited for the champ himself!

At the end of the night, team Stallone ordered a few

Elaina, Sylvester Stallone, and Jenna. PHOTO: MICHAEL SIMON

Sly being presented with the Golden Cannoli. PHOTO: MICHAEL SIMON

desserts for the table. At this point Elaina had a genius plan. We grouped all of our waitstaff who were working that night (twenty-five in total) and had them wait in Fresco on the Go. We gathered all of our famous desserts and sparklers and gave each of the anxious servers one to carry. We waited as the final preparations were being made in the kitchen for this grand parade. With a few seconds to go, the music outside lowered and the entire restaurant began to wonder what was about to happen.

Trumpets blared from the speakers as the introductory salute from the Rocky theme song, "Gonna Fly Now," came on. Upon realizing the champ was in the building, all of our customers looked around. Jenna, Rosanna's daughter, exited from Fresco on the Go with a sign saying, "Welcome Sly!" followed by our parade of team Fresco, each holding a dessert with sparklers. A spotlight moved slowly past all the tables to the Stallones. People were clapping and singing along. Everyone rushed to meet Sly, who was already on his feet pumping his fists up in the air as if he had just completed that run up the stairs to the Philadelphia Museum of Art. Everyone circled around him as the celebration continued. It was quite the spectacle, but there was still one item left to present.

From the kitchen came the celebrated golden cannoli. This massive cannoli weighs about eight pounds and needs to be held with two hands. Rocky took the cannoli and lifted it over his head like the world championship belt. With that final celebration, the parade ended, and we allowed the Stallones to enjoy their dessert and the rest of the evening.

This evening was a great success, and Sly and all of Fresco's guests had a wonderful time. It was an unforgettable night. After all the craziness, Sylvester was kind enough to take photos with a few people, including some of the staff. He thanked us for this welcome and left with a large smile on his face. We know he'll be remembering this time for the rest of his life, as we will too.

CELEBRITY BITES

The Clintons

In 1996, Fresco by Scotto was hosting a fundraiser that Hillary Clinton was to attend. The day before the event, the First Lady's advance team arrived to scout the restaurant. We were informed that Hillary would most likely enter through the side entrance that led into the basement of the restaurant, where a lot of prep work is done for the kitchen. The Secret Service also mentioned she would use the bathroom in the basement before seeing her guests. This realization threw us into a tizzy because the employee bathroom was most definitely not ready for a First Lady. In less than twenty-four hours, the bathroom received a full makeover: it was painted, had new mirrors installed, and even had artwork hung in order to be ready for Hillary; however, she never used it. When the event was over, she exited through the basement and spent a few minutes chatting with our family. We thanked her for coming but mentioned we were disappointed about one thing. We showed her the new and improved bathroom, and she complimented our design and thanked us for making the effort. The bathroom is still renovated today, and our employees can thank Hillary for the upgrade. Hillary did take our Veal Osso Bucco back to Washington, and we believe she shared this delicious dish with the president, since Hillary and Bill have been returning to Fresco ever since.

A few years later, in 2002, Bill and Hillary returned with a group of fourteen to celebrate their wedding anniversary. They had a great dinner, and the restaurant was filled with excitement. At the end of the dinner, we served them a famous dessert we used to have on the menu: Praline Ice Cream Cookie Sandwiches filled with cinnamon ice cream. We wanted to present the dessert properly for the two of them because they were sitting across from each other at this dinner. We put seven ice

Elaina, President Clinton, Rosanna, Anthony Jr., Hillary Clinton, Dad, and Mom.

cream sandwiches, stacked, in front of Bill and the same display in front of Hillary. We had candles for both of them, and, once they had blown them out, planned to distribute the cookies to the other guests. On Hillary's side, the guests were each given a dessert. On the other side, thinking the entire display was for him, the president began to eat *all* the cookies in front of him. These sandwiches weren't little, either! We watched for a moment, stunned, and then had one of our captains run into the kitchen to get six more sandwiches for the guests on his side of the table. Clearly, the Clintons were fans of our food.

In June 2021, Fresco by Scotto hadn't been open for more than two weeks when we received word that former President Bill Clinton wanted to come for dinner that evening and sit outside. We were ecstatic and looked forward to his arrival. It was going to be a beautiful evening, and our new outdoor lemon grove structure is stunning during sunset. The former president was over at 30 Rockefeller Plaza promoting his new book, *The President's Daughter*, which he coauthored with James Patterson. He was going to come over to us right after his interview with NBC. We expected that he would show up with a security detail in an SUV, as he usually did. We were mistaken.

Elaina, President Clinton, and Rosanna. PHOTO: MICHAEL SIMON

An hour or so before his reservation time, Elaina noticed a massive group of around fifty people was heading toward the restaurant. We assumed this was a tour group making its way down 52nd Street, but as they approached, we saw none other than former President Clinton at the front. He had left 30 Rock and walked the three city blocks from the plaza to Fresco. Along the way, he had collected this large group of followers, who took up most of the sidewalk. We were blown away. Not many celebrities or former politicians decide to just walk places unless they're surrounded by twenty security guards. We and everyone on the street were shocked. Paparazzi lined both sides of the sidewalk, snapping photos of the procession as it headed to Fresco. The former president approached our hostess stand with a smile, asking if he could squeeze in forty or so more chairs at his table. Along with his jokes, he couldn't have been nicer: socializing with those who had followed him and the staff, and even signing a few autographs for people who could come up with a pen and paper. He was an incredibly jovial presence at Fresco. He sat at the table for a good hour before former First Lady Hillary Clinton and two friends joined him for their meal. As the sun began to set beyond the horizon, they sat down to a dinner filled with Fresco favorites: Zucchini and Potato Chips, Grilled Pizza Margherita (page 98), Fresco by Scotto's Signature Meatballs (page 161), the works.

This visit of the Clintons was extra special for us. Our father, Anthony, was a *huge* fan of the former president, not to mention a staunch Democrat. Dad was outside Fresco waiting to greet the former president. We thought he was just being a superfan of Bill, but we learned that Dad wanted to be there because he knew this was *the* defining moment that showed the restaurant had made it. The Scottos had risen above all the challenges, questions, and changes of the past twenty-nine years of operation. Now, at this moment, a former president had brought a massive number of people to Fresco's front door. Dad looked out at the entire restaurant with a smile on his face, proud that the new Fresco was a definitive success. President Clinton was a pleasure: he spoke with Dad and took photos with the whole family. This memory was important not only to Dad but to the whole family, since Dad passed two months after President Clinton's visit.

CELEBRITY BITES

Barry Manilow

We've had our share of celebrities who have dined at Fresco. In the past, being new to this life, we were very reluctant to go over to their table. Now we are a party scene—a place to be seen. When people walk in the door, we try to give them an unforgettable experience as if they had just stepped inside the famous Copacabana—which brings us to this next story.

Rob Shuter, host of the ever-popular *Naughty but Nice* podcast, called us to say that Barry Manilow and his lifelong writing partner, Bruce Sussman, were in town and coming to Fresco for dinner. Once again, a light bulb went off in Elaina's head for a grand idea: Let's get "Copacabana" on the playlist and treat Barry to a conga line. Who doesn't enjoy a conga line?

Barry and Bruce came and sat, and as soon as they were comfortable, Elaina went around the restaurant to round up diners who might want to participate in the surprise. We all love to sing along to Barry's hit songs, and "Copacabana" from 1985 remains a favorite. To Elaina's surprise, almost 90 percent of the customers that night were "Fanilows" (die-hard Barry Manilow fans). It couldn't have been a more perfect crowd.

The stage was set. Soon the lights dimmed, and the bongos of Barry's "Copa" came through the speakers. Bruce and Barry were seated in an oval banquette facing outward, swaying and tapping their feet to their hit. We had about thirty people, including Mama Scotto, conga-lining and singing their way through the dining room up to Barry's table. Barry's smile lit up the room when he saw and heard the conga line approaching—his eyes got

Barry Manilow, Rosanna, and Bruce Sussman.

wide and he clasped his hand to his mouth in total surprise. It was a riot! Everyone was laughing, singing, and dancing along. Those who weren't up dancing with us were grooving in their seats.

At Barry's table, the parade kept singing and dancing for one more chorus, and when the song died down Barry and Bruce applauded the group of serenaders. Barry got up and socialized with the guests, being incredibly friendly and gracious to the Fanilows. Like many of the celebrities we have mentioned, he was so appreciative of the love and recognition that we showed him. The "Copa" conga line will be waiting for Barry when he returns to Fresco.

CELEBRITY BITES
Kevin Hart and Chris Rock

It's always a great day when you receive a phone call that Chris Rock and Kevin Hart want to come to Fresco. They were looking forward to a delicious meal and would be filming at our restaurant to promote their comedy tour. The two comedians booked out Fresco on the Go for the evening. We originally thought that it was going to be a party to kick-start their tour; however, it was a more intimate and reserved evening for Chris and Kevin.

When we got the news that they planned to film at On the Go, we made sure to get the space into proper "camera-ready" form. We moved all the tables around, pulled the curtains, and dimmed the lights, making it a more intimate setting. The new Sunset Lounge, Fresco on the Go's alter-ego after lunch hours, is really a beautiful place to spend an evening after a long day at work. It has hip vibes, perfect for having a drink or sharing a pizza. It was a lovely setting for these two friends to catch up.

When the clock reached 7:30 p.m., Rosanna came by, and we began to roll out the red carpet as best as we could. Soon the two comedians showed up. They were kind and polite and made a few jokes with Rosanna, who professed her love for them. They hung out outside of On the Go for a few minutes so that we could take a couple of photos with them and even a promotional video of us all dancing on the sidewalk. Usually when people see us dancing, they sprint to join us, which happened. But Chris and Kevin were still on the clock and had to film, so any more dancing had to wait.

Inside On the Go, it looked like an old-school club where you might find men smoking cigars and having drinks. It was quite the sight. Hart and Rock were talking about life and the tour with each other, while cracking a few jokes in between. They were served dishes of lamb, vegetables, mashed potatoes, creamed spinach, and pasta, and many of Fresco's other famous dishes throughout their talk. To top it off, we presented them with the massive cannoli, which they had a good laugh about. The night ended with the two of them cracking the pastry with tiny golden hammers.

Rosanna, Jenna, Kevin Hart, and Elaina.

Rosanna, Chris Rock, Jenna, and Elaina.

CELEBRITY BITES

Housewives

Countess Luann, Rosanna, and Elaina. PHOTO: Michael Simon

Living in New York City, you never know who you're going to run into. We're fortunate enough that we get to live in the same area as some of our favorite celebrities: The Real Housewives of New York City and New Jersey.

These women, whom we knew even before they were Bravo stars, have been serious and loyal Fresco customers. Our patrons love seeing them while they dine. Seriously, who doesn't want to watch Joey Gorga or Margaret Josephs drink and dance? They have some serious moves.

On some nights Ramona Singer, whom we've known for years and have bumped into on our European vacations, has been dancing on our sidewalk and in the restaurant. It's always a good time when a Bravo housewife shows up. We've been lucky enough to get to know Countess Luann when she debuted her new nonalcoholic Frosé Rosé at Fresco. If anyone knows anything about cocktails, it's these women, and Fresco's new cocktail menu is a big hit with the Housewives.

Rosanna, Melissa and Joe Gorga, and Elaina. PHOTO: Michael Simon

Next Generation

Our children grew up in the restaurant, and it soon became an extension of our homes. Three generations of the Scotto family have worked at Fresco over the past thirty years. Our mom, Marion, would be up front at the hostess desk to greet customers. Her eyes were trained on making sure everything was in its place and our guests were treated like royalty. Our dad, Anthony, sat a few feet aside to offer any additional support in greeting, but let Marion do the work. It's her place, after all. Whenever our kids arrived, Pa and Gram were always there to welcome them with a big hug and a plate of food. However, running a restaurant isn't cheap, so we made sure to put our kids to work.

Our children have all worked for Fresco in some capacity. From the age of sixteen onward, they have been dishwashers, line cooks, prep workers, bussers, waiters, and hosts. During the summers, if our kids weren't at camp or away from home, they would be down in the kitchen learning what it takes to run Fresco. It was nice to have our children as a part of the team and given some responsibility—besides, they were cheap labor. All of them were paid and learned the value of a dollar. There are no free passes for our kids. Learning the importance of hard work and the key points of hospitality was part of every day of their employment.

Jenna, being the first grandchild, was the test-run for this endeavor. She started working as a hostess at Fresco, part-time, at age sixteen. This job requires the hostess to be available and ready from 11:30 a.m. to 1:30 p.m. to handle the lunch rush. One of our favorite Jenna stories is of the time when she got hungry in the middle of lunch service and disappeared into the kitchen to ask the chef to make her a pasta, leaving Mom to run the desk alone.

Our Chefs in Training.

L.J. washing dishes at Fresco.

Jenna thought it was quick, but by the time she returned, lunch was over. She had missed the lunch crowd but not her own lunch. Mom was angry, and Jenna didn't have a clue why Gram was so upset.

Soon Rosanna's son L.J. was in the kitchen working as a potato peeler and artichoke cleaner. Over a few summers, he worked his way up to bus boy, where, not too sure of how to approach tables, he would bow before approaching to serve or clean the tablecloth. At Fresco we treat guests like royalty, but L.J. was taking it too far!

Elaina's son Danny started his career at Fresco on the Go as a barista and cashier. Danny was shy and introverted and was reprimanded multiple times for not being cordial with the customers, which caused him to be demoted to ice-tea maker. Ice teas were handed out for free, so he did not need to mingle with customers. He just needed to be fast.

Since the restaurant relaunched, our children have come back to work for us in some capacity. Elaina's daughter Julia worked as a hostess for a few months over the summer until she returned to her study abroad program at NYU in Madrid. Rosanna's son L.J., worked at Fresco on the Go, coordinating the different parties hosted at the new Sunset Lounge. Jenna is a hostess during lunch and dinner, and you can find her outside greeting customers with her smile from ear to ear. She has been responsible for working alongside our head Chef Ben in retrieving, transcribing, and entering all the recipes in this cookbook. She's also the editor-in-chief of social media for Scotto Sisters and Fresco by Scotto and is a constant guest on our live Instagram. Needless to say, she is being groomed for a starring role at the restaurant. Elaina's son,

Danny (DJ Fauce), is our amazing resident DJ Tuesday and Wednesday for the dinner crowd. He reads the crowd and chooses the perfect songs to set the mood and get everyone dancing after dessert—a far cry from the introverted kid who was demoted years ago! Danny has also authored his debut novel, *Clarity*, and worked with us

Jenna, Danny, and L.J.

Julia and Danny at the DJ booth. PHOTO: MTC PHOTOGRAPHY

spending countless hours interviewing Mom, Rosanna, and Elaina to write the beautiful stories you have read throughout this book. He and Jenna have been the dynamic duo who coordinated for months with the family and editor to hit the quick deadlines for this book's publication. Mama Scotto is so excited to be working alongside the third generation of Scottos at Fresco.

We're all lucky to say that we get to work with family, and we know that whatever the next steps are for the next generation of Scottos, it will be amazing!

Meatballs, Mangia & Memories

Our Favorite Scotto Family Recipes

Appetizers

GRILLED PIZZA MARGHERITA • **98**

EGGPLANT AND ZUCCHINI PIE • **100**

BAKED RICOTTA DIP WITH CROSTINI • **102**

ELAINA'S TOMATO BRUSCHETTA • **105**

GOAT CHEESE AND PROSCIUTTO PINWHEELS • **106**

MINI LENTIL BURGERS • **107**

PROSCIUTTO-WRAPPED ASPARAGUS WITH PARMESAN CHEESE • **108**

MOM'S STUFFED MUSHROOMS • **109**

CHICKPEA ALLA FRESCO DIP • **110**

COD PUREE DIP • **110**

CANNELLINI BEAN DIP • **112**

HOUSE-MADE RICOTTA WITH LEMON ZEST DIP • **113**

FRITTO MISTO • **115**

PIZZA RUSTICA • **116**

Grilled Pizza Margherita

Makes 12 pizzas

DOUGH

1 quart lukewarm water

1 teaspoon fresh yeast

1 tablespoon molasses

2½ tablespoons kosher salt

1¾ cups extra-virgin olive oil

3 cups all-purpose flour

3 cups high-gluten flour

½ cup whole wheat flour

TOPPING

1 cup Pecorino Romano cheese

1 cup grated Bel Paese cheese

1 cup tomato sauce

6 tablespoons chopped fresh parsley

½ cup chopped fresh basil

For the dough: In a mixing bowl, combine water, yeast, and molasses. Mix together gently until all yeast dissolves. Set mixture aside for 5 to 10 minutes, or until yeast makes a raft and bubbles. Stir in salt and 1 cup of olive oil.

With mixer on a low speed, add three kinds of flour. Mix until all flour is absorbed and dough pulls away from side of bowl. Roll dough into one large ball and let stand for 5 minutes.

Cut dough into 12 pieces. Roll pieces into balls and place on an oiled baking sheet. Brush balls lightly with olive oil and cover with plastic wrap. If you are going to use dough right away, let it sit at room temperature for 30 minutes before baking. If you don't need it immediately, you can store it for one day in refrigerator, but you must then let it sit at room temperature for 1 hour before using.

For the topping: In a bowl, combine the cheeses. Have at hand the tomato sauce, parsley, and basil.

To assemble each pizza: When dough is ready, prepare the *fuoco*, or fire—preferably a charcoal fire, but a gas grill works nicely too. Make sure grill is set at least 4 inches above fire.

Grilled Pizza Margherita, cont.

On an oiled surface, flatten out a piece of dough using the palms of your hands. If dough is sticking, lift it and drizzle a little more oil on surface. Dough should be a paper-thin 12-inch circle. The shape of the pizza is not as important as the thickness of the dough.

Gently lift dough and, being careful not to tear it, drape it onto the hot spot of the grill. Dough will start to rise immediately. After about 2 minutes, carefully lift an edge to check color of the underside. When it is an even golden brown, flip pizza over and place it on the side of the grill or a cooler spot of the grill.

Brush cooked side with olive oil. Spread 2½ tablespoons of cheese mixture evenly to edge of pizza. Next, with a tablespoon, drop 8 to 10 dollops of tomato sauce on pizza—but don't spread sauce over whole surface. Drizzle pizza with 1 tablespoon of extra-virgin olive oil and sprinkle with ½ tablespoon of chopped parsley.

Carefully slide pizza back to edge of hot section of grill and rotate it for 3 to 4 minutes until bottom is an even golden brown. Do not put pizza directly over fire, because the bottom will burn before cheese melts.

Garnish with chopped basil and serve immediately.

Eggplant and Zucchini Pie

Serves 6–8

CHEESE FILLING

2 pounds fresh ricotta cheese

2 pounds fresh mozzarella cheese

½ pound Parmesan cheese, grated

¼ cup fresh parsley, chopped

4 eggs

Salt and pepper, to taste

2 large eggplants

4–5 large zucchinis

Salt

4 cups all-purpose flour

10 whole eggs

4 cups bread crumbs
   (store-bought Panko also works)

1½ cups Parmesan cheese, grated

¼ cup fresh parsley, chopped

Salt and pepper

2 quarts extra-virgin olive oil,
   as needed

5 cups tomato sauce

First prepare the cheese filling. In a large bowl, combine ricotta, mozzarella, Parmesan, parsley, and eggs. Mix well and season with salt and pepper to taste. Refrigerate briefly to make mixture firm.

Having all remaining ingredients at room temperature will make for much faster and more even cooking. Slice eggplants and zucchini into approximately ¼-inch-thick slices. Set zucchini aside. Salt eggplant fairly well to remove water; let it sit for 1 hour or so to remove bitter taste; and then pat dry.

Place flour in a shallow bowl. In a second bowl, beat eggs with a fork until blended. In a third bowl, mix bread crumbs, 1 cup Parmesan, parsley, salt, and pepper. Line up bowls on a work surface.

One at a time, carefully dip eggplant and zucchini slices first into flour, making sure both sides are covered, then into egg mixture, and finally into bread-crumb mixture. Coat both sides well and gently tap off any excess coating. Transfer to a large plate and season with salt and pepper.

Chef's Trick! Keep one hand for dry mix and one hand for wet items—otherwise you'll be breading your hand.

Eggplant and Zucchini Pie, cont.

In a large heavy skillet over medium heat, heat enough olive oil for frying. Starting with eggplant, add eggplant and zucchini to skillet and sauté on both sides until golden brown (about 3 minutes), making sure that slices are cooked all the way through and soft. Avoid crowding the pan. Place cooked eggplant and zucchini on paper towels to drain off excess oil, add a pinch of salt to each piece, and pat dry.

Preheat oven to 450°F. In a large 9 × 13-inch baking pan, add 1 cup tomato sauce (or enough to cover bottom of pan); then add a layer of one-fourth of eggplant and zucchini slices; and top with a layer of one-fourth of cheese filling. Repeat process three more times, or until desired height or thickness is reached. Top with a layer of tomato sauce and sprinkle with ½ cup Parmesan.

Bake for 20 minutes, or until golden brown on top. Serve immediately.

Baked Ricotta Dip with Crostini

Serves 6–8

Who doesn't love cheese? This easy-to-make recipe is the ultimate comfort food and will keep you out of the kitchen.

- 2 pounds whole-milk ricotta (Polly-O or any dry ricotta is best)
- 2 cups mozzarella cheese, diced small
- 10 ounces Parmesan cheese, grated
- 1 ounce fresh oregano, chopped
- Pinch of red pepper flakes
- Salt and pepper, to taste
- Crostini (for serving)
- Garlic Sauce (for serving)

Preheat oven to 400°F. Grease a 2-quart (or larger) oval baking dish with olive oil.

In a large mixing bowl, combine ricotta, mozzarella, 8 ounces of Parmesan, oregano, red pepper flakes, salt, and pepper. Mix thoroughly. Form mixture into a football shape and place in oiled baking dish. Top with remaining 2 ounces of Parmesan and bake for 20 minutes, until well browned on top.

To serve, spread baked ricotta over slices of crostini and drizzle garlic sauce over top.

CROSTINI

- 1 round loaf Italian bread
- ½ cup olive oil
- 2 cloves garlic, peeled and cut in half

Preheat oven to 450°F. Slice bread into ½-inch-thick slices. Using a pastry brush, coat both sides of each slice with olive oil and rub each slice with garlic. Place on a cookie sheet and toast in top rack of oven for 3 minutes on each side, or until bread is golden brown on both sides.

GARLIC SAUCE

- 6 tablespoons olive oil
- 3 tablespoons garlic, sliced
- ¼ cup parsley, chopped

Mix olive oil and garlic in a small pan. Cook over medium heat until garlic becomes a light golden brown and then add parsley. Remove from heat and set aside.

Elaina's Tomato Bruschetta

Serves 4-6

5-6 medium tomatoes

2-3 tablespoons of garlic-infused olive oil, plus more or coating and drizlilng

2-3 tablespoons white balsamic vinegar

Basil

Salt

Pepper

Leftover loaves of crusty bread (country bread or baguette bread work best)

Parmesan cheese, grated

Chop tomatoes well (pieces don't need to be perfect or even close—just give them a good chopping) and toss with equal parts of garlic-infused olive oil and white balsamic vinegar; add basil, salt, and pepper to taste.

Cut bread in thick slices (to your preference). Coat both sides of each slice with garlic-infused olive oil and salt and pepper. Sprinkle with grated Parmesan.

Broil until golden brown. Keep a close watch—they brown quickly!

Top each slice with tomato mixture, drizzle with more garlic oil, and *mangiare!*

★ To make the garlic oil, add 1 cup of olive oil and 7–8 cloves of garlic to a small saucepan and turn heat to medium. (Heat settings vary, so keep an eye on garlic. It should cook at a very soft simmer or boil and, depending on saucepan size, you may need to flip garlic cloves.) Allow garlic to cook in oil until golden. Set aside to cool and then strain.

Chef's Trick! Keep garlic for any preparation you want, such as spreading on bread for added depth and extra flavor.

Goat Cheese and Prosciutto Pinwheels

Serves 4–6

- 1 pound goat cheese
- ½ pound Parmesan cheese, grated
- 3 tablespoons toasted pine nuts, chopped
- Salt and pepper, to taste
- 12 thin slices prosciutto
- 2 red peppers, roasted* or jarred
- 2 green peppers, roasted* or jarred
- 2 yellow peppers, roasted* or jarred
- 1 ounce box of long toothpicks

Mix together goat cheese, Parmesan, and pine nuts. Season with salt and pepper to taste if needed.

Cover each slice of prosciutto with a layer of cheese mixture, add a layer of peppers, and season with salt and pepper. Place on a piece of plastic wrap, and roll up tightly to secure; refrigerate for about 1 hour, or until firm.

When firm, remove plastic wrap, slice into 1-inch-thick rounds, and serve on a long toothpick.

If roasting peppers, cut peppers into quarters and remove seeds and membrane. Cook, skin side up, under broiler until skin blackens and blisters. Remove from oven, place in a large metal bowl, and cover with plastic wrap. When peppers have cooled, peel away skins.

Mini Lentil Burgers

Serves 4–6

1 cup (medium size) onion, chopped fine

1 cup garlic cloves, crushed well

1 cup small leeks, finely sliced

1 cup small carrots, finely grated

Salt and pepper

4 cups dry brown lentils

1 cup seasoned Italian bread crumbs or Panko

2½ cups egg yolks

2 tablespoons oil

10–12 mini brioche rolls, or 4–6 larger burger buns

In a pan lightly coated with oil, slowly cook the onion and garlic until tender, season with salt and pepper, and lay on a tray or plate to cool. Do the same with leeks and carrots.

Put lentils in a large pot with lightly salted water and bring to a boil. Reduce heat to a simmer, cover pot, and cook for 25 to 30 minutes, or until lentils are tender. Drain well.

In a food processor, combine half of the cooked lentils with the onion and garlic. Blend until mixture forms a smooth paste.

Transfer to a bowl and add the remaining lentils, leeks, carrots, bread crumbs, and egg yolks. Mix thoroughly, season with salt and pepper, and form the mini burgers just slightly larger than 1 tablespoon or in a size that is just a touch larger than the rolls you bought.

Heat some oil in a large skillet and, working in batches, fry the mini burgers until browned on both sides. Repeat for remaining mini burgers. Place on paper towels to drain.

Serve with warm mini brioche buns and tomato relish or ketchup.

Prosciutto-Wrapped Asparagus with Parmesan Cheese

Serves 4–6

24 jumbo asparagus spears, 4 inches long, bottom removed

8 ounces butter, melted

8 ounces Parmesan cheese, grated

12 slices prosciutto, cut in half

Cracked black pepper

1 lemon, juiced

¼ cup chopped parsley (optional)

Preheat oven to 350°F. Prepare a large baking dish brushed with melted butter.

Bring a pot of lightly salted water to a boil, add asparagus, and blanch for 1 minute, or until just tender.

Drain asparagus and pat dry. Brush spears with melted butter and then roll them in grated Parmesan. Wrap each asparagus spear in one-half slice of prosciutto.

Align asparagus spears one layer deep in baking dish. Sprinkle with Parmesan and cracked black pepper to taste. Bake for 6 to 8 minutes.

Squeeze fresh lemon juice over asparagus, add a light dusting of chopped parsley, and serve.

Mom's Stuffed Mushrooms

Serves 6

24 white button mushrooms

⅓ cup extra-virgin olive oil

2 cloves minced garlic

½ cup dry seasoned bread crumbs (Mom loves 4C!)

Salt and pepper, to taste

1 cup mozzarella, in bite-size cubes

Preheat oven to 400°F and grease a baking sheet with butter or olive oil.

Remove stems from mushrooms and wash in cold water and salt. Drain and pat dry with paper towels.

In a skillet with a thin layer of olive oil, sauté garlic for about 3 minutes. Add bread crumbs, salt, and pepper, and sauté until light brown.

Fill mushroom caps with bread-crumb mixture and top with a small cube of mozzarella. Drizzle with olive oil. Bake for 20–25 minutes or until mushrooms are brown and cheese is melted.

Serve alone or over salad.

Chef's Trick! Make sure your mushrooms are dry before stuffing! Mushrooms are mostly water, so they're susceptible to becoming waterlogged.

Chickpea alla Fresco Dip

Serves 6–8

4 cups dry chickpeas

Salt

1 cup tahini

3 lemons, zested and juiced

Pepper, to taste

4–6 tablespoons olive oil

4–6 tablespoons ice water

Soak chickpeas overnight in a medium-size pot; cover them with more than double the volume of water.

Strain chickpeas, cover with fresh water, and season with salt. Bring pot to a boil, and then turn down to a simmer; cook until the chickpeas are very soft.

Strain chickpeas well and let cool to room temperature. Process in food processor and add tahini, lemon juice, and lemon zest; season with salt, pepper, and olive oil. Add water as needed for consistency, and adjust flavors with salt and pepper to taste.

Serve right away or refrigerate until needed.

Cod Puree Dip

Serves 6–8

2 quarts whitefish (baccalà) puree

1 cup heavy cream
  (more or less, depending on dryness)

Salt, to taste

White pepper, to taste

NOTE: If you can't find whitefish puree, check your local bagel shop or old-school delicatessen.

Add whitefish puree to food processor and slowly drizzle in cream until a mousse is formed. Taste for salt (it should need very little) and add white pepper to taste.

Serve right away or refrigerate until needed.

Cannellini Bean Dip

Serves 6-8

4 cups dry cannellini beans

Salt

1 cup tahini

3 lemons, zested and juiced

Salt and pepper, to taste

2-4 tablespoons olive oil

4 tablespoons ice water

Soak beans overnight in a medium-size pot; cover them with more than double the volume of water.

Strain beans, cover with fresh water, and season with salt. Bring pot to a boil and then turn down to a simmer; cook until beans are very soft.

Strain beans well and let cool to room temperature. Process in food processor and add tahini, lemon juice, and lemon zest; season with salt, pepper, and olive oil. Add water as needed for consistency and adjust flavors with salt and pepper to taste.

Serve right away or refrigerate until needed.

House-Made Ricotta with Lemon Zest Dip

Serves 6–8

1¼ pounds ricotta

3 lemons, zested and juiced

1 cup parsley, chopped (plus more to finish)

¼ pound Parmesan cheese, grated

4 tablespoons olive oil (plus more to finish)

Salt and pepper, to taste

Get the driest ricotta you can get. If it seems wet, use a cheesecloth to strain overnight.

In a large mixing bowl, combine ricotta, lemon zest, lemon juice, parsley, Parmesan, and olive oil. Add salt and pepper to taste. Mix well.

Serve immediately, finishing with a drizzle of olive oil and more chopped parsley. If not using immediately, place in a suitable container and refrigerate until needed.

Fritto Misto

Serves 4–6

- 21 shrimp, size 16/20 per pound, cleaned entirely (head off, tail off, back cleaned)
- 1 pound calamari, tubes and tails cleaned, cut into ¾-inch rings
- 1 pound baby octopus, washed well
- Milk for soaking
- Oil for deep frying
- 2 cups flour
- 3 tablespoons salt for flour, plus more for post-frying
- 2 tablespoons smoked paprika
- 1 medium zucchini, julienned on a mandoline into thin strips

Soak all seafood in milk overnight. Strain well, but do not rinse off. Preheat deep fryer at 350°F.

Add salt and paprika to flour. Combine all seafood in flour and dust thoroughly. Allow to sit and then re-dust with flour for an even coat. Dredge zucchini strips well in flour and set aside.

Add seafood to preheated deep fryer, and 30 seconds later add floured zucchini. Allow to fry for about 1 to 2 minutes or until golden brown.

Place fry in a bowl to drain on paper towels. Let dry and salt to taste.

Pizza Rustica

Makes one 10 × 15-inch pizza

DOUGH

6 cups all-purpose flour, plus more as needed

¼ teaspoon salt

1 pound chilled salted butter, cut into large pieces

5 large eggs, beaten

1¼ cups ice water

FILLING

12 ounces prosciutto, diced small

8 ounces soppressata, diced small

8 ounces mozzarella, diced small

8 ounces provolone, diced small

2 pounds ricotta

4 ounces grated Pecorino Romano

10 large eggs, beaten

1 teaspoon pepper

1 large egg, beaten, for brushing crust

For the dough: In a large bowl, whisk together flour and salt. Using a pastry cutter, large fork, or two knives, cut butter into flour until mixture resembles coarse crumbs. Add eggs and stir for 1 minute. Add ice water, a little at a time, to form a cohesive dough. Knead dough on a lightly floured surface until it forms a large smooth ball, about 5 minutes. Cover with plastic wrap and set aside for 30 minutes.

For the filling: Mix the meats, cheeses, eggs, and pepper in a large bowl.

To assemble: Heat oven to 350°F. Divide dough into two pieces: two-thirds for bottom crust and one-third for top crust. On a lightly floured surface, roll out larger portion of dough into a rectangle to line the bottom and sides of a 10 × 15-inch glass baking dish, with some overhang. Add filling and smooth top lightly. Moisten edges of dough with a little water.

Roll out remaining dough to cover top of dish with some overhang. Trim off excess dough and crimp edges to seal. Poke several sets of holes across the top with a fork or knife. Bake for 45 minutes. Remove from oven and brush top and edges with beaten egg; then return to oven until golden brown, another 45 minutes. Let pie cool completely before serving.

Soups and Salads

ZUPPA DI PESCE • **118**

LENTIL SOUP • **119**

SEAFOOD STEW OR "CIOPPINO" • **121**

SUMMER SALAD WITH RASPBERRY VINAIGRETTE • **122**

RASPBERRY OR RED WINE VINAIGRETTE • **123**

SHRIMP WITH WATERMELON AND TOMATO SALAD • **124**

BEET SALAD WITH TOASTED PISTACHIOS AND CITRUS VINAIGRETTE • **126**

Zuppa di Pesce

Serves 6

- 4 tablespoons olive oil
- 1 carrot, diced small
- 1 red onion, diced small
- 1 stalk celery, diced small
- 2 leeks, cleaned and diced small
- 1 fennel bulb, diced small
- 1 16-ounce can tomatoes, with juice
- 1 teaspoon spicy red pepper flakes
- 1 teaspoon dried oregano
- 2 cups dry white wine
- 1 16-ounce can clam juice
- Salt, to taste
- 2 tablespoons chopped garlic
- 1 1-pound filet sea bass, cut into 4 pieces
- 12 large shrimp, peeled and deveined
- 20 Manila clams (or cockles)
- 1 pound calamari, cleaned and cut into slices
- 12 mussels, cleaned
- 1 cup cooked cannellini beans
- 8 unpeeled red and yellow tomatoes, diced
- 2 tablespoons chopped fresh basil

In a large sauté pan over medium heat, heat 2 tablespoons of olive oil. Sauté carrot, onion, celery, leeks, and fennel for 5 minutes. Add canned tomatoes and cook for 10 minutes. Add red pepper and oregano. Add wine and stir over medium heat for 10 minutes. Add clam juice and cook over medium to low heat for 15 to 25 minutes, or until the flavors are melded and sauce thickens slightly. Add salt to taste.

In another large sauté pan over low heat, sauté garlic in remaining 2 tablespoons of olive oil for 2 minutes, or until golden brown. Pan-sear sea bass for about 5 minutes, turning once, until golden brown on each side, and set aside on a plate. Add the shrimp to pan and sauté 1 minute. Add clams and calamari and sauté 1 minute (clam shells will not open yet). Add mussels and sauté 1 minute. Add reserved sea bass and sauce and cook 5 to 10 minutes over low heat, or until clams and mussels open and soup reaches desired consistency. Add extra clam juice if soup seems too thick.

Warm cannellini beans over low heat and drain before serving.

Garnish soup with with diced tomatoes, cannellini beans, and chopped basil.

Lentil Soup

Serves 8

¼ cup extra-virgin olive oil

4 Italian sausage links, cut into ½-inch rounds

1 large carrot, peeled and diced small

¼ cup minced onion

2 garlic cloves, smashed and minced

1 celery stalk, peeled and diced small

1½ cups crushed canned tomatoes

1 pound dried lentils

8 cups water

Salt and freshly ground black pepper

Heat olive oil in a large soup pot or Dutch oven and sauté sausage over medium heat, until brown, about 5 minutes.

Add carrot, onion, garlic, and celery and sauté until onions are translucent, about 5 minutes. Add crushed tomatoes, lentils, and water and season with salt and pepper to taste. Cover and simmer for 1 hour, or until lentils are tender.

Seafood Stew or "Cioppino"

Serves 4–6

This hearty dish is a great way to cook a variety of seafood. Most of the cooking happens in one pot, so it's not too fussy. This stew is good for a colder day in autumn or winter.

3 1½-pound lobsters, cleaned

1 pound mussels, cleaned

1 pound Manila clams, cleaned

1 pound large shrimp, cleaned and deveined

1½ pounds fish (salmon or halibut), diced medium

1 pound calamari, cleaned

½ cup extra-virgin olive oil

3 cloves garlic, minced

1½ cups onion, chopped

1 cup bell pepper, chopped

2 cups red wine

1 28-ounce can crushed tomatoes

2 quarts tomato juice

2 quarts fish stock or shellfish stock

Bouquet garni of bay leaf, parsley, and basil, wrapped in a layer of cheesecloth and secured with kitchen string

Salt and pepper, to taste

½ cup minced parsley, for garnish

Cook lobsters in boiling, salted water for 4–6 minutes. Cool in ice bath. Drain and split. Set aside.

Steam mollusks (mussels and clams) in a small amount of water (about 2 cups) until they just open. Strain and reserve cooking broth. Set mollusks aside.

Split shrimp shells down the back and remove black vein. The easiest way to do this without removing the shell is to lay the shrimp on its side and insert a small knife into the large end of the shrimp with the blade pointing outward from the back (away from the shrimp and your hands).

Once all seafood is clean, preheat a large saucepan on medium-high heat, lightly coat bottom of pan with olive oil, and add garlic, onion, and bell pepper. Allow to sauté for 3–4 minutes until all ingredients become aromatic.

Add red wine and allow to reduce by half. Then add broth from mollusks, tomatoes, tomato juice, fish or shellfish stock, and bouquet garni and bring to a boil.

Now add shellfish and seafood and allow to simmer for 5 minutes, adding water if needed. Adjust seasoning with salt and pepper, and garnish with parsley.

Summer Salad with Raspberry Vinaigrette

Serves 4-6

8 ounces lola rosa lettuce

8 ounces gem lettuce

2 pints strawberries, cleaned and cut in quarters

1 small yellow squash (4 ounces), cut in quarters and sliced thin

6 radishes, sliced very thin across

2 sprigs oregano, picked and chopped fine

1 shallot, chopped fine

1 cucumber (5 ounces), sliced thin across

2 cups Raspberry Vinaigrette (page 123)

Grana Padano cheese, grated, for finishing (Parmesan can be substituted)

Toss together leafy greens, strawberries, squash, radishes, oregano, shallot, and cucumber with Raspberry Vinaigrette. Garnish with grated cheese.

Summer Salad with Raspberry Vinaigrette, cont.

RASPBERRY OR RED WINE VINAIGRETTE

1 cup raspberry or red wine vinegar

3 cups olive oil (a 75/25 blend with canola oil also works)

3 shallots, minced well

1 tablespoon fresh thyme leaves, picked and chopped semi-coarsely

1 tablespoon fresh oregano leaves, picked and chopped semi-coarsely

1 tablespoon salt

1 tablespoon fresh cracked pepper

1 cup mustard (optional)

Mix all ingredients in a suitable container and shake well before using. Keep refrigerated for up to 10 days.

If you want an emulsified vinaigrette, use mustard. Put all ingredients in a blender and buzz on high for a few seconds—voilà!

Shrimp with Watermelon and Tomato Salad

Serves 4–6

30 shrimp, size 16/20 per pound, fully cleaned, vein removed

Salt and pepper

Olive oil

1 large red watermelon, seedless, diced medium

1 medium yellow watermelon, seedless, diced medium

15 mint leaves, chopped fine

2 pints cherry tomatoes, cut in half (use heirloom mix for extra color!)

1 cucumber, split in half and cut into small half moons

1½ cups Red Wine Vinaigrette (page 123)

1 cup balsamic glaze*

Ricotta salata, grated fine

Olive oil, for finishing

Clean shrimp (head off and clean vein). Season with salt, pepper, and olive oil. Pan sear on medium-high heat until cooked through.

Combine diced watermelon, chopped mint leaves, cherry tomatoes, and cucumbers in a large mixing bowl. Season well with Red Wine Vinaigrette; add salt and pepper to taste.

To plate: Strain watermelon, tomatoes, and cucumber mix and place on a suitable platter. Pour balsamic glaze and sprinkle grated ricotta salata over the salad. Finish with olive oil. Place shrimp decoratively around salad before serving.

★ Balsamic Glaze Alternative

If you don't have access to balsamic glaze, mix 2½ cups balsamic vinegar with 1 tablespoon sugar in a saucepan. Bring to a boil while stirring and then turn heat down to a simmer and reduce mixture until it is approximately 1 cup. (If you over-reduce the mixture, add a few drops of water at a time until it reaches the "syrup" consistency.) Cool and hold until later.

Beet Salad with Toasted Pistachios and Citrus Vinaigrette

Serves 4–6

- 3–4 pounds medium-size red beets or yellow beets, washed thoroughly
- 1 quart red vinegar (for red beets), or 1 quart champagne vinegar for yellow beets
- 1 cup sugar
- 1 cup salt
- 3 sprigs thyme
- 1 sprig rosemary
- 4 bay leaves
- 1½ cups toasted pistachios, plus more for finishing
- 2 tablespoons coriander seeds
- 1 cup Citrus Vinaigrette (page 192)
- 3 cups mâche lettuce
- Salt and pepper, to taste
- 8 ounces goat cheese, crumbled
- Olive oil, for garnish
- ½ cup parsley, chopped, for garnish

Place beets, vinegar, sugar, salt, spices, pistachios, and coriander seeds into a large pot and cover with water. Taste water for seasoning; it should be very sharp and aggressive. Beets do not absorb aromatics well, so if it tastes soft, add more vinegar.

Once seasoning is correct, bring pot to a boil and then turn down to a simmer for 30 to 40 minutes. Allow to cook until beets are tender, so a small knife or cake tester can easily glide through them with little resistance. Remove beets from pot; allow to cool slightly and then peel while warm. Slice one-quarter- to one-third-inch thick and hold until needed.

Assembly: Place sliced beets on a large platter until it is shingled with beets (alternate colors if you cooked both kinds). Lightly dress beets with some Citrus Vinaigrette.

In a small bowl, dress lettuce with remaining Citrus Vinaigrette, seasoning with salt and pepper as needed. Distribute lettuce over beets, sprinkle pistachios around the top, and crumble goat cheese over all to finish.

Garnish with olive oil and chopped parsley. Serve and enjoy!

Pasta

SUNDAY SAUCE WITH MEATBALLS, SAUSAGES, AND PORK CHOPS • **129**

HOMEMADE PASTA • **130**

PENNE PASTA PRIMAVERA • **131**

CAPELLINI WITH MUSHROOM RAGÙ • **132**

LARRY'S LEMON CAPELLINI PRIMAVERA • **134**

ROSANNA'S SPAGHETTI ALLA NERANO • **136**

PESTO PASTA WITH POTATOES • **137**

PASTA BOLOGNESE • **138**

RAVIOLI WITH BROWN BUTTER SAGE SAUCE • **139**

TAGLIOLINI WITH CRAB RAGÙ • **141**

TOMATO SAUCE • **143**

RIGATONI WITH SHORT-RIB RAGÙ • **144**

RICOTTA GNOCCHI WITH TOMATO SAUCE • **146**

GARGANELLI WITH BROCCOLI RABE AND SAUSAGE • **148**

AMATRICIANA • **149**

PAPPARDELLE WITH PESTO GENOVESE • **150**

RISOTTO WITH LOBSTER, SHRIMP, AND CALAMARI • **152**

RISOTTO WITH WILD MUSHROOMS • **154**

Sunday Sauce with Meatballs, Sausages, and Pork Chops

Serves 8–10

- ½ cup extra-virgin olive oil
- 1 pound mild sausage
- ½ pound hot Italian sausage
- 6 thinly sliced pork chops (about 3 pounds)
- 2 cups dry red wine
- 2 tablespoons garlic, chopped
- 2 onions, diced
- 1 cup pancetta, diced
- 1 tablespoon crushed red pepper
- 1 gallon canned Italian plum tomatoes, undrained
- 2 cups fresh basil, chopped
- 2 pounds cooked Signature Meatballs (page 161)
- 2 pounds uncooked rigatoni pasta

In a large stock pot over medium heat, heat oil and sauté sausages and pork chops until brown, about 10 minutes. Don't worry if meat is not cooked through, because it will finish cooking in sauce. Remove meat from pot and set aside. Keep pan over medium heat and deglaze it by adding 1 cup of wine and scraping up the bits.

In the same pot, add garlic, onions, pancetta, and crushed pepper and cook until onions and garlic are lightly browned, about 2 minutes. Add remaining 1 cup of red wine and cook until the mixture is reduced by half. Add tomatoes and simmer for 1 hour over low heat.

Add basil, sausages, pork chops, and meatballs to the tomato sauce, and simmer for 1 more hour over low heat.

In a large pot of boiling, salted water, cook pasta for 10 to 12 minutes or until al dente. Drain pasta, toss it with Sunday Sauce, and serve immediately.

Homemade Pasta

A super-simple recipe that you can make at home.

Serves 4-6

1 pound (3 cups) all-purpose flour

4 whole eggs, beaten

1 pinch salt

2 tablespoons olive oil

Pile flour on a clean worktable or countertop and make a well in the center. Add remaining ingredients to the well.

With your fingers or a fork, lift flour from edges of pile and let it fall into egg mixture until it sticks together and a mass is formed. Continue kneading everything together until a cohesive mass is formed. When you press your thumb into the dough, it should bounce back a little bit.

Place a damp towel over dough and allow it to rest for about an hour. Then follow any instructions on how to make your desired pasta. Some of the easier ones to make at home with a rolling pin and bench knife are pappardelle, fettuccine, pici, large farfalle, and gnocchi.

Unless you're an expert, don't look for perfection. Have fun!

Chef's Trick! Dampen a towel, twist it to make a ring, and place a medium-size mixing bowl in that for stability. Add flour to bowl and mix pasta as described.

Super Chef's Trick!! Put all ingredients in a food processor, buzz until the mixture resembles coarse meal, and then remove and start kneading it into a cohesive mass until very firm. Allow the dough to rest under a damp towel for at least 1 hour, and then you're ready to roll!

Penne Pasta Primavera

Serves 4-6

- 2 pounds dry penne pasta
- 6 tablespoons extra-virgin olive oil
- 3 cloves garlic, minced
- 8 ounces button mushrooms, quartered
- 2 cups small broccoli florets, blanched
- 1 cup frozen peas
- 5 small zucchini, quartered lengthwise and cut to 1-inch lengths, blanched
- 1 cup Parmesan cheese, grated
- 4 tablespoons unsalted butter
- Kosher salt and pepper, to taste
- 2 cups baby red tomatoes, cut in half
- 4 tablespoons basil, thinly shredded (or more to brighten it up)
- ½ cup pine nuts, lightly toasted (optional)

Cook pasta in boiling water with a pinch of salt and a dash of olive oil, until al dente.

Heat 5 tablespoons of olive oil in a 12-inch skillet over medium heat. Add two-thirds of garlic and cook until golden, about 2 minutes. Add mushrooms and cook until golden, about 3 minutes. Add broccoli, peas, and zucchini and cook for 3 minutes. Add cooked pasta, Parmesan, and butter. Season with salt and pepper and toss to combine. Transfer to a serving dish.

Bring remaining olive oil and garlic plus tomatoes and basil to a simmer over medium heat. Pour over pasta and garnish with pine nuts. Enjoy!

Capellini with Mushroom Ragù

Serves 6–7

1 clove garlic, sliced

2–4 tablespoons olive oil

12 ounces of cooked mixed mushrooms

1 cup mushroom stock

1 large shallot, sliced thin

Pinch of chili flakes

4 cups fresh spinach

4–6 tablespoons white wine

4 tablespoons butter

2 pounds dry capellini pasta

4–6 tablespoons Parmesan cheese, grated

Salt and pepper, to taste

Olive oil, for garnish

Sauté garlic in olive oil over medium-high heat until almost golden brown. Add pre-cooked mushrooms and stock, shallot, and chili flakes. As garlic starts to brown, add spinach and toss lightly. Then add white wine to deglaze all ingredients together. Reduce by half, add butter, and allow to simmer.

Bring a pot of lightly salted water to a boil and cook pasta for just 2 to 3 minutes (capellini is a quick-cooking pasta—be careful). Drain pasta, add to sauce, and allow it to finish cooking in sauce for 1 minute. Toss pasta in sauce and remove from heat.

Add Parmesan to create the "cremosa," or creamy, sauce that makes this dish. Add salt and pepper to taste. Add olive oil and more Parmesan on top as desired, and enjoy.

Chef's Trick! A little truffle oil is a great addition at the end.

MIXED MUSHROOMS AND STOCK

12 ounces of cooked mixed mushrooms (Hen of the Woods, King Oyster, button mushrooms)

Olive oil

Salt

White wine

Slice cleaned mushrooms and sauté in olive oil, seasoning with salt. Remove from pan when golden brown. Cover entire bottom of pan with white wine. Continue cooking to reduce and lift remaining "fond," or caramelized bits, from the pan. Add approximately 1⅓ cups water to create stock.

Chef's Trick! Make mushroom stock with dry mushrooms. Cover ¼–⅓ pound dry mushrooms with 2 quarts water and boil for 45 minutes to 1 hour, until it reduces to about 2 cups of mushroom stock. Strain well and reserve until needed. Save mushrooms for the pasta as well.

Larry's Lemon Capellini Primavera

Serves 6–8

- 2 pounds dry capellini pasta
- 6 tablespoons olive oil
- 4 large bulbs of garlic, peeled and sliced thin
- 1 teaspoon chili flakes
- 1–2 cups white wine
- 10 pieces of Lemon Preserves
- 1 bunch (1½ pounds) asparagus, cut into 1-inch lengths, blanched
- 1 large zucchini, diced and blanched
- 1 yellow squash, diced and blanched
- 6 tablespoons butter
- Salt, to taste
- Pepper, to taste
- 3 cups Parmesan cheese, grated
- Lemon Gremolata, for garnish
- 1 cup parsley, chopped, for garnish
- Olive oil, for garnish

Cook pasta in boiling water with a pinch of salt and a dash of olive oil, until al dente. Strain, saving some of the water, and set aside.

In a large sauté pan, add olive oil and garlic. Sweat garlic until light brown, add chili flakes, and then deglaze with white wine.

After wine has been reduced by half, add lemon preserves, pre-blanched asparagus and squashes, butter, and salt and pepper to taste. Lastly off the flame, add 2 cups of Parmesan; add more if sauce feels too thin.

Once sauce is where it should be (it should coat the back of a spoon), reheat pasta (unless it is still warm). Add reheated pasta to pan along with an ounce or two of pasta water to coat pasta and keep it from drying out. Stir to combine with vegetable mixture.

Plate pasta and top with remaining Parmesan, Lemon Gremolata, parsley, and olive oil.

Chef's Trick! Using lemon oil instead of olive oil to garnish the pasta will kick the flavor up a little.

Larry's Lemon Capellini Primavera, cont.

LEMON PRESERVES

2 cups simple syrup*

3 lemons, sliced across in very thin rounds (a mandoline works best, but watch your fingers!)

Bring simple syrup to a boil and pour over lemon slices. Allow to sit for 6 hours.

* To make simple syrup, bring 1 cup sugar and 1 cup water to a strong boil, stirring to combine thoroughly.

LEMON GREMOLATA

1 cup bread crumbs (or Panko)

3 tablespoons butter

Zest of 4 lemons

2 tablespoons chopped parsley

Fry bread crumbs with butter in a skillet, keeping the pan moving constantly. Add lemon zest when bread crumbs are light to medium dark brown, and add parsley at the very end. Mix well and place on a tray lined with paper towels; allow to cool for later.

Rosanna's Spaghetti alla Nerano *Recipe adapted from Lo Scoglio.*

Serves 6

- Grapeseed oil for frying
- 3 yellow squash and 3 zucchini (approximately 2 pounds), sliced in ¼-inch-thick rounds
- Salt
- 2 pounds spaghetti
- Olive oil
- Salt, to taste
- Black pepper, to taste
- Unsalted butter, to taste
- 1½ cups Grana Pedana cheese, grated
- 1 bunch fresh basil leaves, chopped (or whole, for rustic), for garnish

Heat a generous amount of grapeseed oil in a large, deep saucepan. Use a thermometer if possible; oil should be 325–350°F.

Fry squash and zucchini slices in hot oil until they begin to turn golden. Drain slices with a slotted spoon, place in a bowl, season with salt, and refrigerate overnight or at least 2 hours to rest and soften.

When you are ready to prepare dish, bring a large pot of salted water to a boil and cook spaghetti until al dente. Once it is cooked to desired doneness, strain pasta (reserving some of cooking water), splash lightly with olive oil, and let cool until needed.

Heat rested squash and zucchini in a large frying pan along with two small ladles of spaghetti cooking water. Season with a pinch of salt, freshly ground black pepper, and some butter.

Remove pan from heat and add a couple handfuls of grated Grana Pedana and a spoonful of butter. Toss everything together well, garnish with basil, and enjoy!

Pesto Pasta with Potatoes

Serves 4–6

Forget the food coloring—this crowd pleaser hits every mark for Saint Patrick's Day! We love this dish all year round. It's healthy, delicious, and tastes great at room temperature.

1 pound fusilli pasta (any dry pasta will work!)

6 ounces Yukon gold potatoes, diced small

Extra-virgin olive oil

Parmesan cheese, grated

In salted water, cook pasta and potatoes separately until pasta is al dente and potatoes are tender. Reserve a cup of salted cooking water.

In a medium-size saucepan, add pesto to pasta and potatoes. Slowly add cooking water and toss mixture over medium-low heat. Drizzle with extra-virgin olive oil and top with Parmesan. Give mixture a few more tosses and then plate.

Chef's Trick! Garnish with toasted pine nuts for some crunch and even more grated Parmesan for some added creaminess!

PESTO

3 cloves garlic, sliced thin

2 tablespoons pine nuts

½ cup Pecorino Romano or Parmesan cheese, grated

4 cups basil (about 1½ bunches)

½ cup extra-virgin olive oil

Kosher salt

In a food processor, pulse garlic with pine nuts until a paste is formed. Add cheese and slowly add basil along with olive oil. Add salt to taste and blend until smooth.

Chef's Trick! Use half Parmesan and half Pecorino Romano. It gives you the best of both worlds—salty and creamy!

Pasta Bolognese

Serves 4–6

- 1 medium onion, coarsely chopped
- 1 large bulb fennel, coarsely chopped
- 1 large carrot, coarsely chopped
- ½ cup olive oil
- 1 teaspoon crushed red pepper flakes
- 3 large garlic cloves, finely chopped
- 1 pound ground chicken
- 1 pound ground beef
- 2 cups tomato sauce
- 1 cup white wine
- 2 cups beef stock
- Salt and freshly ground black pepper
- ¼ cup butter
- ½ cup Parmesan cheese
- Pinch of red pepper flakes

In a food processor, grind onion, fennel, and carrot until very, very fine.

In a large saucepan, heat olive oil over low heat. Add ground vegetables, pepper flakes, and garlic, and simmer, stirring occasionally, for about 30 minutes or until moisture evaporates.

Remove vegetables from pan, leaving a little remaining olive oil, and then add ground chicken and beef to same pan, turning to mix and cook. When meats are brown, add tomato sauce, wine, and stock to saucepan. Return vegetables to pan, stir everything together, and simmer over medium to medium-high heat, stirring occasionally, for 1½ hours or until sauce thickens and is reduced by one quarter. Season to taste with salt and pepper.

Serve over your favorite pasta, adding butter, Parmesan, and pinch of red pepper flakes to combined pasta and sauce.

Ravioli with Brown Butter Sage Sauce

Serves 4

- 2 boxes ravioli (check serving size on package)
- ¾ cup unsalted butter
- 1 clove garlic, chopped and crushed
- ¼ cup fresh sage leaves, coarsely chopped (or whole for more rustic)
- ⅓ teaspoon ground black pepper
- Kosher salt, to taste
- Fresh lemon juice (optional)

Cook ravioli following instructions on the package.

Melt butter in a medium saucepan set over low-medium heat. When butter begins to get just slightly bubbly, add garlic. Stir garlic in butter for 1 minute. Add sage to garlic butter and continue stirring for 2 to 4 more minutes, until butter has turned very light brown and has a rich, nutty aroma. (It is very easy to burn this sauce, so keep stirring and don't step away.) Season sauce with ground black pepper and salt.

Remove sauce from heat and transfer to a bowl to keep it from burning. Add a spritz of lemon juice if desired. Add sauce to cooked ravioli and serve.

Tagliolini with Crab Ragù

Serves 4–6

1½ cups crab stock (page 142)

6 cloves garlic, sliced

Olive oil

Split crab backs, for garnish (optional)

Pinch of dried oregano

Red pepper flakes, to taste

Salt and pepper

2 cans plum tomatoes, chopped, with juice

2 ounces (about 1 bunch) fresh basil leaves, chopped

5 ounces frozen peas, thawed out

8 ounces lump crabmeat

2 pounds dry tagliolini pasta (or make your own!)

2 tablespoons butter (optional)

Prepare crab stock ahead of time.

In a large sauté pan, sauté garlic in olive oil over medium-high heat for 1 minute, until golden brown.

Add split crab backs (if desired for garnish), oregano, red pepper flakes, and salt and pepper. Continue to sauté for 5 minutes.

Add crab stock to mixture and simmer for 4 minutes.

Add canned tomatoes with juice. Stir and bring to a boil and then lower heat and continue to stir until sauce has been brought to a simmer. Cover and cook for 45 minutes. Add basil and remove from heat. Stir in thawed-out peas. At the very end, add lump crabmeat. Season to taste.

Boil pasta in water for 8 to 10 minutes (follow instructions on package) until al dente, and strain.

For a more velvety sauce, add butter to pasta, incorporating butter thoroughly, before adding sauce. To serve, add pasta to a soup bowl and top with sauce.

Chef's Trick! Place a crab back on each bowl, or two or three crab backs on a platter for an over-the-top garnish.

Tagliolini with Crab Ragù, cont.

CRAB STOCK

3 pounds blue crabs, cleaned and split

½ cup extra-virgin olive oil

2–3 cups white wine (leftover wine works)

2 tablespoons garlic, chopped

½ pound large carrots, diced

½ pound large celery, diced

½ pound large onions, diced

2 cans plum tomatoes, chopped, with juice

6 tablespoons tomato puree or tomato paste

1–1½ gallons water

Add crabs to a large cooking pot with oil. Stir crabs well, legs and all. Sauté for 3 to 4 minutes, add white wine, and bring to a boil.

Once the shells have a light color, add garlic, carrots, celery, onions, canned tomatoes with juice, tomato puree or paste, and water. Allow to simmer for 2 hours.

Buzz very well with a stick blender and strain carefully.

Chef's Trick! Ask your seafood purveyor to split and remove crab backs; these can be used for garnish. If crab backs are separated, toast them in an oven at 300°F for 5 minutes, and rinse well.

Alternative Crab Stock

Buy 1½ quarts premade fish or clam juice, fish stock, or lobster stock. Reduce to 3 cups and add canned tomatoes. The mixture will be a little darker than the first method.

Tomato Sauce

Serves 3–5

1 cup olive oil

1 cup garlic, sliced

2 cups basil, chopped

1 teaspoon chili flakes
 (a little less if you're sensitive to spice)

3 quarts canned peeled plum tomatoes
 (San Marzano tomatoes if you can find them!)

Salt and pepper, to taste

Pour olive oil into a large pot, allow to warm, add garlic, and cook until garlic starts to turn a light brown. Then add half of basil and chili flakes and allow all ingredients to begin to fry. Before everything turns black, add canned tomatoes and stir all ingredients together well. Turn heat down to medium-low (a light simmer).

Allow to simmer for about 2 hours, stirring often. Once sauce has been simmering and tomatoes have broken down, add remaining basil and chili flakes.

Using a stick blender, blend until you have a smooth tomato sauce and everything is incorporated well. Taste for seasoning and let cool until needed.

Rigatoni with Short-Rib Ragù

Serves 6–8

1 gallon veal stock, reduced by half

2 pounds short ribs (chuck flap)

Salt and pepper

Oil

1 cup garlic, shaved (save half for serving)

1 cup shallots, sliced

10 sprigs thyme

1 sprig rosemary

2 cups red wine

1 quart tomatoes, chopped

1 cup cherry tomatoes (optional)

1 cup basil, chopped

2 pounds rigatoni pasta (or paccheri)

½ cup parsley, chopped, for finishing

Olive oil, for finishing

Parmesan cheese, grated, for finishing

Preheat oven to 300°F. Warm veal stock to a light simmer.

Season short ribs liberally with salt and pepper (seasonings tend to come off in searing process). Heat oil on medium-high, in an oven-proof pot of suitable size, until a light smoke comes off pot. Place short ribs in pot and sear well (a dark brown or crimson color starts once all sides are browned). Remove short ribs from pot.

Add half of garlic, shallots, thyme, and rosemary to pot. Once all are incorporated well, add wine and turn heat to high for a moment to cook out alcohol and reduce by half.

Put short ribs back into pot. Then add veal stock, cover pot, and place in oven for 3 hours.

Remove pot from oven and use tongs to remove all ribs. If you want to shred the meat, now is the time! The short ribs should be *very* tender, so you can shred them with a fork. For a more rustic dice, allow short ribs to cool and then cut into cubes.

Strain liquid that remains in pot. Add it back to pot along with tomatoes, basil, and remaining half of chopped herbs. Reduce liquid by half and then combine with short ribs. Refrigerate until needed.

Rigatoni with Short-Rib Ragù, cont.

To serve, pre-cook pasta. Have one pot of water heated and ready for reheating pasta.

Slowly warm ragù in a pan of suitable size until it reaches a light simmer.

Briefly put pre-cooked pasta in boiling water, strain out, and add to ragù, incorporating everything together well.

Once mixed well, plate on individual plates or on a platter, finish with parsley, olive oil, and Parmesan, and enjoy!

Ricotta Gnocchi with Tomato Sauce

Serves 4–6

- 1 cone (3 pounds) ricotta cheese
- 1 quart Parmesan cheese, grated
- 3 eggs
- 4½ cups flour, plus 1 cup for rolling and adjusting consistency
- 1 tablespoon black pepper
- 1 cup Tomato Sauce (page 143)

Place all ingredients in a bowl and mix gently until incorporated into a cohesive mass. Refrigerate for at least 2 hours.

Once mixture is cool, flour your worktable. Using a medium-size kitchen knife, cut ricotta mixture into manageable pieces and, with both hands, roll it out into logs a little smaller than the diameter of a quarter (the lengths of the logs don't matter). Then cut logs into sections about 1 inch long. To make ridges, roll sections along the back of a large dinner fork . . . as they do in the old country!

If you want to save gnocchi for later, sprinkle with a little extra flour and freeze.

If you're using gnocchi right away, cook them in a pot with a perforated basket that can be submerged. Bring salted water to a boil, add gnocchi, and give a quick stir. When they are floating, strain them out. Serve with Tomato Sauce or any other favorite sauce.

Garganelli with Broccoli Rabe and Sausage

Serves 6–8

Olive oil for cooking

½ cup onion, diced very small

½ cup fennel, diced small or minced

2 tablespoons fennel seeds, toasted well

2 cups white wine

3 pounds loose Italian pork sausage

1¼ cups garlic, chopped

Salt and pepper, to taste

2 quarts marinara sauce

1 cup basil

2 bunches broccoli rabe, chopped and blanched

Pinch of chili flakes

2 pounds dry garganelli pasta (or any dry pasta)

Butter (optional, for finishing)

In a medium-size pot, warm oil and then add onion, fennel, and fennel seeds, cooking until tender—for about 30 minutes or until all ingredients are translucent *but not browned*. Add wine and reduce by half.

Add pork sausage and garlic and allow to cook until proteins have gone from pink to white. Taste for salt and pepper, and then add marinara sauce and allow to simmer slowly for about an hour. Finish with basil, broccoli rabe, and chili flakes.

Cook pasta in a pot of boiling salted water until al dente, strain, and toss with butter if desired.

Taste sauce for seasoning and then serve with pasta.

Chef's Trick! Sauce can be cooked and stored until needed. Don't forget that ragùs are easy to freeze for later!

Amatriciana

Serves 6–8

This is a very rustic dish! Don't overthink it! Guanciale is already salted, so taste carefully before you salt this sauce. Pecorino pairs with this ragù very well, but Parmesan also works!

- 3 pounds guanciale, sliced ¼ inch thick
- 2 pounds Spanish onion, diced large (2 large onions)
- 6 shallots, sliced thin (⅛ inch)
- 2 cups white wine
- 2 tablespoons chili flakes
- 1 gallon marinara
- 1 cup water (if needed)
- Pepper to taste
- 2 pounds cooked paccheri

Slowly render out guanciale over medium-low heat. When it is fully rendered, add onions and shallots and cook until semi-soft. Remove mixture from pan, add wine, and reduce by half, just to remove trimmings in pan and cook alcohol out of the wine.

Return previous ingredients to pan and add chili flakes and marinara. Allow to simmer for one hour on low. If sauce seems too greasy, add just a splash of water and skim fat off the top. Add pepper to taste. Serve with paccheri or refrigerate until needed.

Pappardelle with Pesto Genovese

Serves 6–8

- 2 pounds dry pappardelle (or any long pasta)
- Olive oil (for cooking and garnishing)
- 2 ounces shallots, sliced fine
- Pinch chili flakes
- 1 cup white wine
- ½ cup butter
- Pine nuts, for garnish
- 6 ounces ricotta, for garnish

Cook pasta in a pot of boiling salted water until al dente, strain, and set aside. Keep a pot of water hot for pasta to be reheated if necessary.

In a large sauté pan, warm a light coat of oil. Add shallots and cook until tender. Add chili flakes and white wine and reduce by half. Then add pesto and allow to warm.

At this point add cooked pasta (re-warm it for a moment in boiling water if necessary) to the sauté pan. Mix pesto and pasta together well. Stir in butter.

Place pasta on a suitable platter or plate, finish with a drizzle of olive oil, a sprinkle of toasted pine nuts, and a few scoops of ricotta on top. Enjoy!

Pappardelle with Pesto Genovese, cont.

PESTO GENOVESE

6 ounces basil
 (approximately 2 large bunches), blanched

6 ounces spinach (dried well),
 blanched

2 cups Parmesan cheese, grated

1 cup olive oil

4 cloves raw garlic
 (boil them if you want less spice)

2 cups toasted pine nuts
 (save some for garnish)

Ice water for blending
 (1 cup on the side)

Salt and pepper, to taste

This way of making pesto is a little less classic but results in a much smoother consistency. If you don't have a blender that can do purees, then a standard food processor will yield similar results.

Blanch 2 bunches of basil leaves in boiling water for about 15 seconds, strain, and place immediately into an ice water bath. Cool well and then strain all excess water.

Blanch 8 ounces of spinach for approximately 10–15 seconds in boiling water, strain well, and place immediately into an ice water bath. Cool well and then dry well.

Put all ingredients *except* the ice water into blender. Turn blender on medium-high and firmly press ingredients into blade, slowly adding ice water until blade grabs all ingredients and a thick puree is formed. Taste for salt and pepper. Chill immediately and hold until needed.

Risotto with Lobster, Shrimp, and Calamari

Serves 10

- 1 cup extra-virgin olive oil
- 2 tablespoons shallots, chopped
- 1 tablespoon garlic, chopped
- 2 cups Arborio or Carnaroli rice, uncooked
- 2–4 cups lobster stock
- 1 cup dry white wine
- 2 cups tomato sauce
- Lobster meat from 3 lobsters, cooked*
- ½ pound shrimp, cooked and cut small
- ½ pound calamari, cooked and cut small
- 2 tablespoons fresh parsley, chopped
- 1 tablespoon fresh basil, chopped
- Salt and pepper

In a pot over medium heat, heat olive oil and sauté shallots and garlic until golden brown. Add rice and stir, making sure to mix risotto well with the oil.

Slowly add 2 cups of lobster stock and wine and simmer for 15 minutes, stirring constantly, making sure that risotto doesn't stick to bottom of pan. As soon as stock is absorbed, continue to add more (2 cups at a time), to keep risotto moist. Cook until risotto has a creamy texture and is cooked through.

Add tomato sauce, lobster meat, shrimp, calamari, parsley, and basil and continue to stir for approximately 5 more minutes. Add salt and pepper to taste. Serve immediately.

* How to Cook a Lobster: In a pot filled with enough boiling water to cover three 2-pound lobsters, cook lobsters for about 5 minutes. Cool down in ice water and then clean them: take off backs with a knife, cut tails in half, crack claws and legs, and take meat out. Set aside shells for lobster stock and meat for risotto.

Risotto with Lobster, Shrimp, and Calamari, cont.

LOBSTER STOCK

3 lobster shells, cooked

3 garlic cloves

1 cup extra-virgin olive oil

1 onion, chopped

1 carrot, chopped

1 celery stalk, chopped

¼ bunch fresh thyme, chopped

¾ cup tomato paste

1 cup dry white wine

8 cups water

In a large stockpot over medium heat, sauté lobster shells and garlic in olive oil for 2 minutes. Add vegetables, thyme, and tomato paste and cook for 10 minutes. Add wine, reduce by half, and then add water.

Bring stock to a boil over high heat, lower to medium heat, and simmer for 30 minutes. Strain and cool liquid; you will have about 4 cups of stock. Set stock aside.

Risotto with Wild Mushrooms

Serves 6

- ½ cup dried porcini mushrooms
- 3 tablespoons butter
- 1 pound wild mushrooms (morels, shiitake, or other), sliced
- Salt and pepper
- 2½ quarts chicken stock
- ½ cup olive oil
- 6 garlic cloves, chopped
- ½ onion, diced
- 2 cups Arborio or Carnaroli rice, uncooked
- ½ cup dry white wine
- ¾ cup Parmesan cheese, grated
- 3 tablespoons fresh parsley, chopped

Soak dried porcini mushrooms in 1½ cups of very hot water for 20 minutes, or until plumped. Drain mushrooms and chop fine. Set aside.

In a sauté pan over medium heat, melt butter and cook wild mushrooms for 3 minutes, or until soft. Season with salt and pepper. Set aside.

In a stockpot over high heat, bring chicken stock to a low simmer.

In a heavy-bottomed pot, heat olive oil and sauté garlic and onion over medium heat until golden brown. Add rice and stir thoroughly. Add wine and porcini mushrooms to pan, stirring constantly.

Add 2 cups of chicken stock and simmer for 15 minutes, stirring constantly to make sure risotto doesn't stick to bottom of pan. When risotto has absorbed stock, slowly continue to add more, 2 cups at a time. The goal is to cook rice and obtain a creamy texture. Add sautéed mushrooms approximately 3 minutes before end of cooking time. Reserve any remaining chicken stock for use in another recipe.

Stir in Parmesan, garnish with parsley, and serve immediately.

Meats

PRIME RIB WITH ROASTED POTATOES AND MUSHROOMS • **156**

FRESCO BURGER • **159**

FRESCO BY SCOTTO'S SIGNATURE MEATBALLS • **161**

RACK OF LAMB WITH CANNELLINI BEAN SALAD
AND LEMON-CAPER SALSA VERDE • **162**

ROASTED HALF CHICKEN WITH MASHED POTATOES • **164**

VEAL MILANESE WITH ARUGULA SALAD • **166**

GRILLED ANGUS SIRLOIN STEAK PIZZAIOLA
WITH SIMPLE ARUGULA SALAD • **169**

BRAISED LAMB SHANKS • **171**

BALSAMIC SKIRT STEAK
WITH SUN-DRIED TOMATO PESTO AND ARUGULA SALAD • **172**

BRAISED SHORT RIBS WITH ROASTED GARLIC MASHED POTATOES • **174**

CHICKEN COTOLETTA WITH ARUGULA AND RED ONION SALAD • **176**

Prime Rib with Roasted Potatoes and Mushrooms

Serves 5–7

2 steaks,
    32-ounce dry aged ribeye steaks
    (or any good-quality steak)

Olive oil

2 tablespoons sea salt,
    plus more for finishing

Freshly ground black pepper

Sprigs of fresh rosemary and thyme,
    for finishing

Have your butcher trim steaks of excess fat (leave a little fat, though, to keep flavor on the steak!). Remove steaks from refrigerator about an hour before cooking and let them come to room temperature to allow for more even and faster cooking.

Condition grill lightly with olive oil. Preheat grill to high temperature for 15 minutes and then lower to medium-high heat. About 10 minutes before putting steaks on grill, season them fairly liberally with salt and freshly ground pepper. Allow seasonings to "burn" or absorb into steaks and then lightly rub with olive oil.

Place steaks on grill over medium-high heat (over one of the hotter areas). Mark them well and turn; once steaks are marked well on both sides, place on second-level rack (or move steaks to a place where temperature is more moderate than high and just keep flipping every 5 minutes or so). Allow steaks to cook with the grill on high until internal temperature is 130–135°F (medium rare/medium) and then remove from grill.

Let steaks rest for 5 minutes before cutting into slices. Then place steaks on a large serving platter, garnish with potatoes and mushrooms, season with sea salt, black pepper, a drizzle of olive oil, and sprigs of fresh rosemary and thyme. Enjoy!

Prime Rib with Roasted Potatoes and Mushrooms, cont.

ROASTED POTATOES AND MUSHROOMS

1 pound medium Yukon Gold potatoes

2 tablespoons extra-virgin olive oil, plus more as needed

1 bulb fresh garlic, smashed

8 ounces wild mushrooms, sliced

Salt and pepper, to taste

2 sprigs fresh rosemary

4 sprigs fresh thyme

In a large pot of salted water, bring potatoes to a boil and then hold at a soft simmer until cooked through. Cool, quarter into wedges, and hold until needed.

Lightly coat bottom of a sauté pan with olive oil and add garlic cloves. When cloves become semi-brown, remove them; then add mushrooms and cook until tender and light brown (don't move mushrooms around too much). Season with salt and pepper at the very end and set aside. (Note that mushrooms can be sautéed ahead of time and added back into the same pan as the potatoes.)

Preheat oven to 375°F. Place potatoes on a large baking sheet with a lip, lined with aluminum. Season with salt, pepper, rosemary, thyme, and a drizzle of olive oil, and bake for 15 to 20 minutes until golden brown. Then combine with mushrooms and serve.

Fresco Burger

Serves 6

4 plum tomatoes, slow-roasted and split in half

Salt and pepper

Olive oil

Fresh rosemary, chopped

Fresh thyme, chopped

2 or 3 shallots, shaved very, very thin

Cornstarch for shallots

Oil for frying

2 slices pancetta

6 12-ounce burger patties (80/20 blend of ground beef)

12 slices provolone cheese

6 large brioche sesame buns

Pickle slices (homemade optional)

1 head of romaine lettuce, sliced very thin (or use full leaves—gem lettuce is a great substitute)

Preheat oven to 275°F. Cut tomatoes in half from top to bottom and season with salt and pepper, a generous amount of olive oil, and chopped rosemary and thyme. Roast in oven for 2 hours; remove once they are cooked and "wilted."

Slice shallots very, very thin, dust well in cornstarch, and allow to sit for 5 minutes. They will "sweat" a little bit (water comes out of them). Re-dust with cornstarch and then fry in oil at 300°F for 2–3 minutes, until golden brown. Remove from fryer oil into a bowl with a paper towel and season with salt; reserve for later.

Preheat oven to 350°F. Slice pancetta into one-eighth-inch slices. Lay on a baking sheet lined with parchment paper and place in oven for 10–15 minutes, checking often and rotating the tray so that slices cook evenly. Remove when desired bacon-like doneness is reached.

Season burger patties well with salt and pepper, brush lightly with olive oil, and place on hot spot on grill until they have a grill mark. Once they have desired char, place on the second rack of grill or oven until a temperature of 130–135°F is reached. As you hit that temperature, place cheese over top of burgers to allow it to melt.

Start building the burgers with pickles, tomatoes, shallots, pancetta, and lettuce.

Chef's Trick! Toast both sides of burger buns and add a touch of butter for added juiciness inside the bun when you toast it. The little things make a big difference!

Fresco Burger, cont.

PICKLES

6 kirby cucumbers

2 cups champagne vinegar

1 cup white vinegar

4 cups water

1 cup sugar

2 cloves garlic, whole

1 sprig thyme, whole

I sprig rosemary, whole

1 bay leaf

1 tablespoon salt

1 serrano (or jalapeño) pepper, split in half

Wash cucumbers and put them in an adequate storage vessel, allowing a little room at the top to add boiling liquid. Bring all ingredients *except* cucumbers to a boil in a suitable pot. Pour boiling liquid with spices over cucumbers (if necessary, use a clean towel or plate to weigh down cucumbers so they are entirely submerged). Allow container to sit out until it reaches room temperature (an hour or so) and then refrigerate for 6 hours before using. These pickles can be stored for weeks!

Chef's Trick! This pickling recipe can be used for cauliflower, green beans, carrots—any vegetables you want to preserve. Note that the larger the vegetable, the more time it will take to pickle.

Fresco by Scotto's Signature Meatballs

Serves 6-9 (depending on your appetite!)

2 cups bread crumbs or Panko

1 cup milk

2 cups white onions, finely chopped (slowly cooked until tender)

Canola or blended oil

2 tablespoons salt

1½ tablespoons finely ground black pepper

5 pounds ground beef

4 eggs, whole or whisked

2 cups provolone cheese, diced small

1 cup Bel Paese cheese, diced small

1 cup Parmesan cheese, grated fine

Soak bread crumbs or Panko in milk for at least an hour, until very soft.

Cook onions in canola oil or a blended oil on low/medium heat until translucent and very tender. Strain any excess oil and season with salt and pepper.

Place ground beef in a mixing bowl. Add milk and bread crumb mixture, which should be a soft, cohesive mass. Add eggs, whole or whisked. Then add all other ingredients. Mix well with a hook attachment (this allows some air in, so mixture doesn't become tough or hard). After mixing for about 10–15 minutes, refrigerate meatball mixture for about an hour.

Preheat oven to 450°F. Scoop or hand roll portions into size you want for meatballs. Place meatballs on a baking sheet or large flat sauté pan and bake for 5 minutes on each side, rotating occasionally to get color on all sides.

Chef's Tricks! Put a little oil on your hands or gloves as you roll meatballs. It makes them less sticky on your hands and helps you make them very round! We use scoops for consistency and portioning. When meatball mixture is cold, it's easier to scoop and form meatballs.

Rack of Lamb with Cannellini Bean Salad and Lemon-Caper Salsa Verde

Serves 6–8

Lamb marinade

- 3 racks of lamb, split in half (6 half racks of lamb)
- Salt and pepper
- Olive oil

Apply marinade to lamb and refrigerate overnight for best results.

Preheat oven to 400°F. Lightly rub off excess marinade and then season lamb with salt and pepper.

In a preheated pan, add olive oil and allow it to heat up to a very light smoke. Add lamb to pan, searing well on all sides.

Once lamb is seared, place pan inside oven for about 10 to 20 minutes (depending on the size, times may vary). Use a meat thermometer and probe the rack of lamb close to the bone; you are looking for 140°F for a medium-rare lamb chop. Once desired temperature is reached, remove lamb from oven, allow to rest for 5 minutes or so, slice, and serve with Lemon-Caper Salsa Verde and Cannellini Bean Salad.

LAMB MARINADE

- ½ cup rosemary leaves, chopped fine
- 2 tablespoons thyme leaves (optional)
- 2 tablespoons garlic, chopped fine
- 1 tablespoon black pepper
- Pinch of salt
- ½ cup olive oil

Place all ingredients except oil into a food processor. Add half of the oil and then turn on processor. Slowly add rest of oil until a loose paste is created.

Rack of Lamb with Cannellini Bean Salad and Lemon-Caper Salsa Verde, cont.

LEMON-CAPER SALSA VERDE

1 cup parsley, chopped

½ cup capers

½ cup olive oil

1 cup lemon oil

Zest of 1 lemon

Pinch chili flakes

Pinch salt

Combine all ingredients and set aside until needed.

CANNELLINI BEAN SALAD

3 cups dry white cannellini beans

2 cloves garlic

¼ cup carrots, diced

¼ cup celery, diced small

¼ cup onion, diced small

Salt

4 bay leaves

4 sprigs thyme

1 bunch large asparagus, blanched and cut into 1-inch lengths

1 lemon, zested and juiced (for finishing)

Olive oil

Salt and pepper

Place beans with garlic, carrots, celery, and onion in a pot of fresh, cold water seasoned with salt, bay leaves, and thyme. Bring to a boil and then turn down to a simmer. Simmer until tender and then strain. Keep some residual cooking liquid to hold beans in until you're ready to make the salad.

Blanch asparagus in a separate pot of water; *make sure to cool it in ice water, or the asparagus will overcook and turn brown.*

Combine beans, asparagus, lemon zest, and equal parts lemon juice to olive oil. Toss well and season with salt and pepper.

Roasted Half Chicken with Mashed Potatoes

Serves 4

2 chickens,
    split in half and marinated

Olive oil

Salt

Pepper

2 pounds Mashed Potatoes

Apply marinade to chicken and refrigerate overnight for best results.

Preheat oven to 400°F. Remove excess marinade from chicken and season with salt and pepper.

In a suitable large sauté pan, heat olive oil on medium-high heat to a light smoke. Place chicken in skin side down and allow to cook for a few minutes.

When skin has started to lightly brown, put pan with chicken into preheated oven for 15 to 20 minutes. Use a meat thermometer if you have one; internal temperature should be 160°F. When desired temperature is reached, remove from oven. Serve over beautifully whipped Mashed Potatoes.

MARINADE

1 cup oregano, chopped

1 cup parsley, chopped

½ cup garlic, rough chopped

Olive oil

Salt

Pepper

Place oregano, parsley, and garlic into a food processor. Add half the oil and then turn on food processor. Slowly add rest of oil until a loose paste is created. Add salt and pepper to taste.

Roasted Half Chicken with Mashed Potatoes, cont.

MASHED POTATOES

2 pounds Yukon Gold large potatoes, peeled, cut into medium 2-inch pieces

6 tablespoons unsalted butter, soft or melted

1 cup heavy cream, warmed

1 cup sour cream (optional)

2 teaspoons salt

White pepper to taste

In a suitable pot, cover potatoes with cold water and bring up to a simmer. Cook until tender and then strain well.

Place potatoes back in pot on low heat and allow steam to cook out of potatoes. You want to remove as much moisture as possible. Once potatoes are dry, mash them with a food mill, ricer, or a handheld potato masher.

When potatoes are mashed well, slowly add butter, cream, and optional sour cream, thoroughly warmed, into the mash, using a rubber spatula or wooden spoon. Season with salt and pepper and serve.

Veal Milanese with Arugula Salad

Serves 4

- 4 10-ounce veal chops, bone in, pounded to about ¼ inch thick
- 3 cups flour
- 12 whole eggs, whisked
- 5 cups bread crumbs (or Panko)
- 3–4 cups oil
- 1 cup butter
- Salt
- 2 cups Parmesan cheese, shaved or grated
- ½ cup parsley, chopped
- 2 lemons, cut in half (optional: grill lemons for extra flair)

For the breading procedure, set up three containers: one for flour, one for egg, and one for bread crumbs.

Chef's Trick! Keep one hand for egg and flour and one hand for the bread crumbs or Panko—or else you'll be breading your hand.

Place each piece of veal first in flour, dusting chop well on both sides; then submerge chop in eggs; and then coat chop well with bread crumbs.

In a medium to large frying pan, heat a half-inch or so of oil to 350°F. (A thermometer works best to check the oil temperature. Butter can be added to control the temperature of the oil.)

Place breaded veal in pan, add one-quarter of butter, and let butter bubble and lightly brown. Move pan constantly to cook evenly, and flip veal about every minute for even coloring. Once veal is evenly colored to a rich brown, remove to a plate lined with paper towels, season with salt, and pat dry.

To serve, place Arugula Salad (page 173) over the corner of the bone of the fried veal chops. Sprinkle grated Parmesan and parsley over salad and chops and garnish each plate with half a lemon.

Grilled Angus Sirloin Steak Pizzaiola with Simple Arugula Salad

Serves 6–8

6 12-ounce Angus sirloin steaks (Ask your butcher what's best!)

Salt and pepper

Olive oil

Pizzaiola Sauce (page 170)

1 cup Parmesan cheese, grated or shaved

Heat up grill or get a hot skillet ready. Season steaks with salt and pepper, and, if grilling, lightly coat steaks with oil. If you're cooking on a stove top, put a light coat of oil in skillet and cook. Flip steaks to cook on both sides for even coloring or marking, until they reach 135°F for medium rare.

Once desired temperature is reached, remove steaks from heat and serve with a good spoonful of Pizzaiola Sauce and Simple Arugula Salad (page 173). Finish all with Parmesan and enjoy!

Grilled Angus Sirloin Steak Pizzaiola with Simple Arugula Salad, cont.

PIZZAIOLA SAUCE

1 large onion, diced small

½ cup shaved garlic

2 large shallots, sliced thin

1 cup red wine

1 cup Castelvetrano olives, cut in half

1 cup capers, smashed

1 teaspoon chili flakes

1 quart marinara sauce

½ cup basil, coarsely chopped

½ cup oregano, coarsely chopped

½ cup parsley, coarsely chopped

Salt and pepper

In a small saucepan, cook onion, garlic, and shallots to a light golden-brown. Then add red wine to deglaze pan and reduce wine by half. Add olives, capers, and chili flakes and allow to cook for 5 minutes. Then add marinara and simmer for about 30 minutes.

Add all herbs and mix well. Season with salt and pepper to taste. Serve while still warm, or let cool and store until needed.

Braised Lamb Shanks

Serves 6

1 gallon chicken stock

6 lamb foreshanks

Salt and pepper

1 pound carrots, diced large

1 pound celery, diced medium

1 large Spanish onion

7 large cloves garlic

4 sprigs rosemary

2 cups red wine

1 cup tomato paste

2 bay leaves

Parsley, chopped
 (optional, for garnish)

Preheat oven to 325°F. In a pot on the stove, bring chicken stock at least to a steam, if not a soft boil.

Season lamb shanks with salt and pepper and sear them well on all sides.

In a large oven-proof pot, add enough oil to coat bottom of pan. Add carrots, celery, onion, garlic, and rosemary, and brown all ingredients well. Once they reach a dark brown color, add red wine to deglaze pan. (There could be a flare-up, so be careful!) Reduce wine by half and stir in tomato paste and bay leaves.

Now add lamb shanks to pot, pour in chicken stock, cover, and place pot in oven for 3 hours. Check after 2½ to 3 hours: the lamb should be tender. If it isn't done, let it cook for another 30 minutes or so.

Once lamb is tender, carefully remove, strain out vegetables, and reduce sauce by about half. When sauce is reduced, place lamb and vegetables over Roasted Fingerling Potatoes (page 194) and glaze well with sauce. Garnish with chopped parsley.

Balsamic Skirt Steak with Sun-Dried Tomato Pesto and Arugula Salad

Serves 5–8

4 large skirt steaks (approximately 3 pounds), cut in half

Steak marinade

Submerge steaks in marinade and refrigerate for at least 6 hours.

Preheat grill to medium-high heat and season grill lightly with oil. Remove excess marinade from steaks and pat dry; then season steaks with salt and pepper and a light coat of olive oil. Mark steaks well on grill and then cook to desired temperature (135°F for medium-rare).

Serve with Sun-Dried Tomato Pesto and Arugula Salad.

STEAK MARINADE

1 quart balsamic vinegar

1 ounce oregano, chopped rough

2 ounces shallots, sliced

Fresh cracked black pepper

Combine balsamic vinegar, oregano, shallots, and a liberal amount of fresh cracked black pepper.

Balsamic Skirt Steak with Sun-Dried Tomato Pesto and Arugula Salad, cont.

SUN-DRIED TOMATO PESTO

½ pound sun-dried tomatoes

½ ounce mint, chopped well or cut in chiffonade

2 cups (approximately) olive oil

Zest of 3 lemons (juice them after!)

Salt and pepper to taste

Rehydrate sun-dried tomatoes in hot water until semi-tender. Strain well and add mint. Slowly drizzle olive oil into tomatoes and stir until a spreadable sauce or "pesto" is created. Finish with lemon zest, salt, and pepper. Refrigerate and reserve until needed.

ARUGULA SALAD

1½-pound bag arugula (or mixed green lettuce)

2 cups cherry tomatoes, cut in half (optional)

1 cup Red Wine Vinaigrette (page 123)

Salt and pepper

Combine arugula and cherry tomatoes in a bowl of suitable size. Add dressing and mix well. Season with salt and pepper.

★*For Simple Arugula Salad, leave out the tomatoes and use ½ cup dressing.*

Braised Short Ribs with Roasted Garlic Mashed Potatoes

Serves 6–8

½ cup olive oil

6 pounds beef short ribs, cut 2 inches wide

Salt and freshly ground black pepper

1 cup prosciutto, diced

1½ cups carrots, finely grated

2 cups onion, finely grated

1 cup fennel (1 trimmed bulb), finely grated

¼ cup garlic, chopped

1 tablespoon lemon zest, grated

1 tablespoon orange zest, grated

1½ cups tomato puree

1 cup red wine

1 cup beef stock

1½ teaspoons crushed red pepper flakes

Preheat oven to 375°F. In a large, heavy skillet, heat oil over medium-high heat. Season short ribs with salt and pepper to taste and put about a third of them into skillet. Sear until browned, 2 to 3 minutes per side. Transfer seared ribs to a large roasting pan. Sear the remaining ribs in batches, taking care not to crowd the pan.

Reduce heat to low, add prosciutto to same skillet, and cook for 10 to 12 minutes, until fat is rendered. Carefully pour off fat and discard, keeping prosciutto in skillet.

Add carrots, onion, fennel, and garlic and cook, covered, for about 20 minutes, or until vegetables soften. Add lemon and orange zest, tomato puree, wine, stock, and red pepper flakes. Season to taste with salt if necessary and cook for about 5 minutes longer.

Pour sauce over ribs in roasting pan. If necessary, add more stock or water so that liquid comes three-quarters of the way up the sides of the ribs. Cover tightly with aluminum foil and roast for 1½ hours. Remove foil and roast for about 1 hour longer, or until ribs are very tender.

Transfer ribs to a warm serving platter. Pour remaining sauce into a saucepan, bring to a boil over medium-high heat, and cook until it is reduced to about 3 cups. Pour sauce over ribs to serve.

Serve with Roasted Garlic Mashed Potatoes (page 175).

Braised Short Ribs with Roasted Garlic Mashed Potatoes, cont.

ROASTED GARLIC MASHED POTATOES

1 cup garlic, chopped

1 tablespoon extra-virgin olive oil

Salt and freshly ground black pepper

2 pounds Idaho potatoes, peeled and cut in quarters

7 tablespoons unsalted butter

1½ cups heavy cream

Spread garlic on a baking sheet. Sprinkle olive oil over garlic and season with salt and pepper to taste. Cover with aluminum foil. Roast garlic at 450°F for 1 hour, or until tender. Let garlic cool and grind it into a paste in food processor.

Place potatoes in a saucepan full of cold water and bring to a boil. Cook for about 20 minutes, or until cooked through. Drain and set aside.

In another saucepan, melt butter over medium-low heat. Add cream and heat until it comes to a boil. Mix in potatoes and garlic and mash to desired consistency. Season with salt to taste.

Chicken Cotoletta with Arugula and Red Onion Salad

Serves 2

2 chicken breasts, 6–9 ounces each (tenderized and thin)

Olive oil

Salt and pepper

Lightly dress tenderized chicken with olive oil, salt, and pepper.

Heat some oil in a frying pan on medium-high heat and sear chicken on one side. When you see pink turning to white on the top side, flip the chicken and turn heat to low.

Drizzle a little olive oil over chicken before serving with Arugula and Red Onion Salad.

ARUGULA AND RED ONION SALAD

1 red onion, finely shaved

1 bag arugula

2 pints cherry tomatoes, cut in half

Salt and pepper

Dressing
  (use anything you like,
  from Caesar to simple balsamic)

2–4 ounces ricotta salata, grated

Soak shaved red onion in water with a pinch of salt for an hour. Drain before adding to other ingredients. Toss onion with remaining salad ingredients in a bowl, seasoning with salt and pepper and your choice of dressing. Shave cheese over salad and enjoy!

Fish

TOMATO-AND-HERB-CRUSTED FILET OF SOLE • **178**

BAKED CLAMS • **179**

MARINATED SEAFOOD SALAD • **180**

PAN-SEARED DOVER SOLE WITH SAUTÉED SPINACH • **181**

GRILLED BRANZINO AND PUTTANESCA SALSA VERDE • **182**

LOBSTER ARANCINI • **185**

PAN-SEARED SALMON WITH SHAVED FENNEL AND ARUGULA SALAD • **186**

PAN-SEARED SALMON WITH KALE AND SQUASH PANZANELLA SALAD • **187**

SEARED SCALLOPS, CITRUS FREGULA SALAD AND CAULIFLOWER PUREE • **188**

Tomato-and-Herb-Crusted Filet of Sole

Serves 4–6

1 pound ripe plum tomatoes

Ice water bath

Extra-virgin olive oil (as needed)

2½ tablespoons garlic, chopped

1 cup toasted bread crumbs (or Panko)

Salt and pepper

½ cup parsley, chopped, plus extra for garnish

4–6 sole filets, 8 ounces each

2 lemons, juiced

1 cup butter

Preheat oven to 350°F and start a pot of boiling water.

To prepare plum tomatoes, remove core and score bottom side of tomato very lightly. Then place in boiling water for approximately 20 to 30 seconds or until skin starts to break. Remove from boiling water and place directly into an ice water bath. Then peel skin, remove seeds, and dice into small pieces.

In a sauté pan, warm olive oil to lightly coat pan, and then add garlic and sauté until it turns a light golden brown. Add bread crumbs and continue to cook until a golden-brown color is achieved. You may need to add a touch more olive oil, as well as making sure that pan is constantly moving and bread crumbs are being tossed around evenly. Then add tomatoes and cook for 30 seconds more. At the very end, add salt and pepper to taste and half of parsley.

To assemble, place filet of sole on a sizzler plate coated with a light layer of olive oil and then sprinkle with parsley, salt, and pepper. Place a quarter-inch (at most) layer of bread-crumb mixture on top of fish. Bake for 10 minutes or until fish is golden brown.

Remove from oven and prepare sauce: mix together juice from fish, a squeeze of lemon juice, butter, the second half of parsley, and salt and pepper.

Garnish with parsley and serve with the sauce.

Baked Clams

Serves 4–6

- 4 pounds littleneck clams
- 1 cup salt
- 3 cups bread crumbs
- ½ cup Parmesan cheese, grated
- 2 lemons, zested and juiced (zest first)
- 2 tablespoons garlic, chopped
- 3 tablespoons pesto (page 137, or store-bought)
- ½ cup parsley, chopped
- ½ cup olive oil
- 4 ounces clarified butter, melted

Preheat oven to 350°F.

Place clams in a bucket of cold water and salt. Soak for 1 hour.

Place bread crumbs, Parmesan, lemon juice, zest, garlic, pesto, parsley, and olive oil in a bowl. Mix together well and add half of clarified butter. Stir until moist, but not too wet (if it seems dry, add a touch of olive oil). Use additional butter only if needed.

Open each clam and place mixture on top. Place in oven and bake for 12 minutes or until golden brown; remove when golden brown. Enjoy!

Marinated Seafood Salad

Serves 6–10

- 2 cups white wine
- 1½ tablespoons black peppercorns
- 3 garlic cloves, sliced
- 2 bay leaves
- 1 lemon, juiced, seeds removed
- 1 2-pound octopus (will shrink)
- 1 pound medium shrimp, peeled and deveined
- 1 pound calamari, cleaned and cut into half-inch rings
- 1 pound lump crabmeat
- ½ cup carrots, julienned
- ½ cup red onions, julienned
- ½ cup celery, julienned
- ½ cup extra-virgin olive oil
- ½ cup garlic, chopped fine
- 2 cups lemon juice
- Pinch of chili flakes
- ½ cup parsley, chopped
- 1 cup orange segments (fresh or canned)
- 1 cup orange juice
- Salt and pepper, to taste

The octopus can be cooked up to two days in advance.

In a large pot, combine white wine, salt, peppercorns, garlic, bay leaves, 1 gallon water, and lemon juice. Bring to a boil and then lower temperature to a simmer. Add octopus incrementally, slowly dipping in one-quarter at a time—repeating about four times per quarter, for 8 to 10 seconds per dip—until octopus is completely submerged. Let simmer for 45 minutes, or until tender. Remove pot from heat and remove octopus from water to a tray lined with paper towels. Allow to cool to room temperature and then refrigerate.

Cook shrimp and calamari together in the same liquid at a slight simmer for 2 minutes (taste one shrimp just to be sure!). Place them in a salted ice bath to cool, and then dry, cover, and refrigerate until needed.

Using the same water, parboil carrots, onions, and celery for 1 minute, or until tender. Drain and cool vegetables.

According to your preference, remove soft purple skin and suckers from octopus or leave them on. Marinate for 1 hour in a mixture of olive oil, garlic, lemon juice, chili flakes, and parsley.

Preheat grill or plancha (griddle) to medium-high. Cook octopus for 10 minutes or until tender with a nice char. Then cut it into quarter-inch pieces. Mix seafood, vegetables, orange segments, and orange juice in a large bowl and let mixture marinate in refrigerator for at least 12 hours before serving. Add salt, pepper, chili flakes, parsley, and olive oil to taste. Serve and enjoy!

Pan-Seared Dover Sole with Sautéed Spinach

Serves 6–8

½ cup olive oil

6 Dover sole filets

Salt

Pinch of white pepper

2 cups white wine

1 cup capers, strained

1 cup butter

½ cup lemon juice

½ cup parsley, chopped

Lightly oil bottom of a large, preheated sauté pan. Place three fish filets top side down in pan and season with salt and white pepper. Allow to lightly brown on one side, then, using a fish spatula, flip fish over.

Now add half of wine to pan (if it flares up, just let it simmer back down). Add half of capers right after, and then add half of butter. Let butter melt down—it will become slightly foamy. At this point you should have an emulsification that is lightly coating fish.

Next add half of lemon juice. Taste for seasoning, and at very end add in half of parsley. Remove fish to a plate. Move pan vigorously to keep emulsion. Spoon sauce from pan over fish.

Repeat cooking process in a separate pan with the other half of ingredients. Serve all with Sautéed Spinach.

SAUTÉED SPINACH

3-pound bag of spinach, blanched and strained well

Olive oil

6 whole cloves of garlic, smashed

Salt and pepper

First blanch the spinach. Submerge in a large pot of boiling salted water for 10 to 15 seconds. Remove with a large slotted spoon or strain in a colander and cool immediately in an ice bath. Press dry and keep cool until needed.

To sauté the spinach, warm up a large sauté pan on medium-high heat and lightly coat bottom with olive oil. Add garlic, and when it has reached a light golden brown, add spinach, spreading it as evenly as possible in pan. Season with salt and pepper to taste. Serve immediately.

Grilled Branzino and Puttanesca Salsa Verde

The salsa verde is a great condiment to put on bread, toss into a pasta with garlic and oil, or even serve with fish (or any meat on hand). You can omit the anchovy if you want— you will just be missing out on a unique layer to the sauce.

Serves 6–8

6 large branzino filets, 1⅓–1¾ pounds each

Olive oil

Salt and pepper

3 lemons, cut in half

Preheat grill to medium-high and lightly rub oil over the grill with a towel or brush.

On a clean plate or tray, season branzino filets with salt and pepper and a light coat of olive oil. Place branzino on grill at a 45-degree angle to create nice hash marks. You should be able to cook each filet on one side all the way through, without flipping. Grill a lemon cut in half for garnish.

When branzino is cooked through, serve over Quinoa Arugula Salad (page 192) and garnish with Puttanesca Salsa Verde.

PUTTANESCA SALSA VERDE

1 cup Castelvetrano olives, chopped

1 cup capers, rough chopped

½ cup boquerón anchovies (marinated in olive oil), chopped

Pinch of cracked pepper or chili flakes

Salt

1½–2 cups olive oil, as needed

½ cup parsley, chopped

Add all ingredients *except* olive oil and parsley to a small food processor. Quickly buzz it a few times until a medium-coarse mix has been made. Put into a small bowl or suitable container and cover with olive oil. Add chopped parsley at the end.

Keep cold and serve as soon as possible. Don't forget there's fish in this spread!

Lobster Arancini

Serves 10–12

Olive oil

5 ounces shallots, chopped fine

1 pound Arborio rice

2 cups white wine

5 cups seafood stock, warmed

3 cups Parmesan cheese, grated

1 pound mozzarella, diced small

1 cup tomato paste

1 pound lobster meat

½ cup lobster roe

Salt and pepper

FOR BREADING

3 cups flour

12 eggs, beaten

6 cups Panko or bread crumbs

In a large rondeau, add olive oil over medium-high heat and then add shallots and cook until translucent. Then add rice and cook for a few minutes, until exterior of rice develops a clear translucence. Cover rice with white wine and allow to reduce. Then add one-third of seafood stock (make sure it's hot). Stir regularly. Once first third is reduced, add second third, stirring regularly. Add tomato paste, lobster meat, lobster roe, and then the last of the stock. Add salt and pepper as needed. Taste to make sure rice is cooked well. Once it is cooked through, add Parmesan, mix well, and let cool.

When rice is cool, use a medium-size scoop (3–4 ounces) to scoop it up into balls. Place a piece of diced mozzarella in the middle of each scoop of rice and roll them into spheres. Put flour in one bowl, eggs in a second bowl, and Panko in a third bowl. Dip each rice ball into flour, then into eggs, and finally into Panko.

Preheat fryer to 350°F. Place rice balls into fryer basket. Fully submerge for 3 to 4 minutes or until golden brown. Strain arancini in fryer basket. Season with salt and enjoy!

Pan-Seared Salmon with Shaved Fennel and Arugula Salad

Serves 6

Olive oil for sautéing

6 pieces salmon, 6 ounces each (skin off or skin on)

Salt and white pepper to taste

Remove salmon from refrigerator about an hour before cooking. Preheat oven to 375°F.

Lightly oil bottom of a large sauté pan and heat until oil starts to smoke. Season salmon with salt and white pepper and place in pan (if skin is on, place skin side down). If fish buckles a little bit, wait 10 to 15 seconds and then apply light pressure with a spatula or spoon to restore contact between salmon and pan.

Once a golden brown skin has been created, flip salmon over and place in preheated oven for 5 to 10 minutes or until it reaches 130°F (medium in temperature).

Serve with Shaved Fennel and Arugula Salad.

SHAVED FENNEL AND ARUGULA SALAD

12 ounces baby arugula

1 large fennel bulb, shaved thin

Segments from 4 oranges

2 medium watermelon radishes, shaved thin

1 cup toasted sliced almonds

1 cup Citrus Vinaigrette (page 192)

In a mixing bowl of suitable size, add arugula, fennel, orange segments, and radishes and mix evenly. Add dressing in parts until entire salad has been lightly coated.

Pan-Seared Salmon with Kale and Squash Panzanella Salad

This variation on a classic panzanella salad is fun for any time of the year— and a good autumn and winter option!

Serves 6–8

Olive oil for sautéing

6 salmon filets, 6–7 ounces each

Salt and white pepper

Lightly oil bottom of a medium to large sauté pan and heat until oil starts to smoke. Season salmon filets with salt and white pepper and place in pan. Sear for about 4 minutes on each side or until desired doneness is achieved. Serve with Panzanella Salad.

PANZANELLA SALAD

1 quart of medium croutons from leftover bread (focaccia or country loaf work well; double amount to make it more authentic)

12 ounces baby kale

6 ounces blanched haricots verts, cut into 1-inch pieces

1 small butternut squash (8–10 ounces), cleaned and peeled into strips

¼ cup parsley, chopped

¼ cup oregano, chopped

1 cup Citrus Vinaigrette (page 192)

In a large mixing bowl, combine croutons, kale, haricots verts, squash, parsley, and oregano.

Add Citrus Vinaigrette and toss to coat.

Seared Scallops, Citrus Fregula Salad, and Cauliflower Puree

Serves 6

30 large scallops, size U8 or U10

½ cup olive oil for cooking

½ cup salt and pepper

½ cup butter

Remove scallops from refrigerator and allow them to come to room temperature for about 20 minutes.

In a medium to large sauté pan on medium-high heat, lightly coat bottom of pan with olive oil. Season scallops lightly with salt and pepper. Once pan is hot, add scallops to pan with flattest side of scallops facing down. When a light ring of brown color forms around scallops, gently lift them and place them back down again. Now add butter and baste scallops for 2 minutes.

When scallops are semi-firm and golden brown on top (or underside), turn heat off. To serve, flip scallops over and arrange with Citrus Fregula Salad and Cauliflower Puree, and enjoy!

Seared Scallops, Citrus Fregula Salad, and Cauliflower Puree, cont.

CITRUS FREGULA SALAD

6 cups cooked fregula
(follow instructions on package)

Seeds of 1 pomegranate

3 large oranges, segmented and juice removed (save all juice)

2 grapefruits, segmented (save all juice)

2 pints cherry tomatoes, cut in half

1 small red onion, shaved very thin

1 cup parsley, chopped

½ cup finely sliced basil

¼ cup chopped mint, optional

3 cups arugula

Olive oil and champagne vinegar for finishing

Salt and pepper to taste

Cook fregula ahead of time. Cool and hold until needed.

Clean and wash all vegetables. Completely deseed a pomegranate. Clean oranges into segments; keep juice and segments together; and do the same with grapefruit. Slice cherry tomatoes in half. Slice onion very fine on a mandoline and rinse with water for a few minutes once sliced; then dry onion slices well.

In a large mixing bowl, combine fregula and all fruits, vegetables, herbs, and arugula. Season with the leftover orange and grapefruit juices, olive oil and champagne vinegar as needed, and salt and pepper.

Keep salad cold until needed; leave out for 30 minutes before serving.

CAULIFLOWER PUREE

Olive oil

1 head cauliflower,
broken into medium-size florets

2 cloves garlic, sliced

2 large shallots, sliced fine

1 quart cream

1 tablespoon butter

Sprig of thyme

Pinch of white pepper and salt

On medium-high heat, lightly coat a large sauté pan in olive oil. Once the pan is warm, add cauliflower and allow to cook well, until it starts to turn a golden brown or crimson color. Add garlic and shallots, stirring well so nothing burns. When shallots and garlic are slightly cooked, add cream until it covers cauliflower and simmer for 15 to 20 minutes.

When cauliflower is tender, strain out cauliflower, garlic, and shallots. Keep cream close by. Put strained cauliflower, garlic, and shallots in a high-speed food processor. While processing, add butter and then add cream back in very small portions until a smooth but thick puree is formed; it should be a light brown color. Taste for salt and pepper.

Sides

QUINOA ARUGULA SALAD WITH CITRUS VINAIGRETTE • **192**

PARMESAN-CRUSTED MASHED POTATOES • **193**

ROASTED FINGERLING POTATOES • **194**

CAULIFLOWER AND ROASTED GARLIC • **195**

HARICOTS VERTS AND TOMATO • **196**

SCOTTO POLENTA • **197**

MAMA SCOTTO'S SAUSAGE AND RICE STUFFING • **198**

Quinoa Arugula Salad with Citrus Vinaigrette

Serves 5–7

3 quarts water (as needed)

2 tablespoons olive oil

1 clove garlic

½ cup carrot, diced large

½ cup onion (small onion cut in half)

1 stalk celery

4 bay leaves

2 cups red quinoa (not cooked)

2 cups white quinoa (not cooked)

1 cup fava beans (or frozen green peas)

3 cups arugula

1 cup Citrus Vinaigrette

Salt and pepper

Bring a large pot of water to a boil and turn down to a simmer.

In another pot of suitable size, coat pot very lightly with olive oil. Quickly sauté all of garlic, carrots, onions, celery, and bay leaves. Add quinoa, toast very quickly (15 to 20 seconds), and then add simmering water to cover all ingredients by about an inch. Season with salt. Allow to simmer until quinoa begins to "pop" (it will look like little blonde shoots coming out). Taste to make sure it is tender. Once tender, strain immediately and allow to cool.

Combine quinoa, fava beans, arugula, and Citrus Vinaigrette, and season with salt and pepper.

CITRUS VINAIGRETTE

Juice of 6–7 freshly squeezed lemons

1 teaspoon Dijon mustard

1 teaspoon honey

½ cup extra-virgin olive oil

Salt and freshly ground black pepper

In a small bowl, whisk together lemon juice, mustard, honey, and olive oil. Season with salt and pepper to taste. Refrigerate after use.

Parmesan-Crusted Mashed Potatoes

Serves 6–8

2 pounds Russet potatoes, peeled and cut into 8–10 medium pieces

Salt

8 ounces melted butter

2 cups heavy cream, warm

2–3 cups Parmesan cheese, grated

Parsley, chopped, for garnish

Olive oil

Ground white pepper

Preheat oven to broil. Put potatoes in a suitable saucepan or pot, add water just to cover, and season with salt. Bring potatoes to a light simmer and let them cook for 30 to 40 minutes. Check with a fork: once they are tender, strain, and allow them to steam for 1 to 2 minutes.

While potatoes are cooking, in a separate small saucepan, warm butter and cream and hold warm to the side.

To get rid of as much water as possible, place potatoes back in pot with heat on, until they have more or less stopped steaming. Then process them in a ricer or a food mill. Next, add about one-third of the hot liquid at a time and stir until potatoes have a smooth, rich consistency. Be careful not to overwork potatoes, as they can become waxy.

Put potatoes in a casserole dish (or even a saucepan) of suitable size. Cover them with Parmesan and place under broiler. *Do not take your eyes off them!* It takes only a few minutes. Once the cheese reaches a golden-brown color, remove from oven and finish with parsley, olive oil, and pepper to taste. Serve as soon as you can!

Roasted Fingerling Potatoes

Serves 6–8

1½ pounds fingerling potatoes

Olive oil

Salt and pepper

Pinch of chili flakes (optional)

¼ cup parsley, chopped

1 sprig oregano, picked and chopped well

Preheat oven to 475°F. Line a baking sheet with aluminum foil (for easy cleaning).

In a bowl of suitable size, lightly oil potatoes, seasoning them with salt, pepper, and a pinch of chili flakes, and mix well. Place on baking sheet and bake in oven for 20 to 30 minutes. Check them regularly for doneness—a small paring knife should glide in and out effortlessly.

When done, remove from oven and place in a suitable bowl. Mix in herbs and taste for seasoning. Serve immediately.

Cauliflower and Roasted Garlic

Serves 6-8

2 heads cauliflower

Olive oil

Salt and pepper

1 cup garlic, sliced

4 tablespoons butter (optional)

1 cup parsley, chopped

Preheat oven to 400°F.

Break cauliflower into small pieces, around the size of a silver dollar. Put smaller pieces in a mixing bowl, lightly coat with olive oil, mix well, and season with salt and pepper.

Put cauliflower on a baking sheet and place in oven. Every 5 minutes, use a spatula to turn cauliflower over so it can roast evenly. When a dark, roasted color is achieved, remove from oven and hold.

On medium-high heat, lightly coat bottom of a large sauté pan with olive oil and add garlic to pan. When garlic starts to turn a light brown, add cauliflower and butter (if using). Mix well. Taste for seasoning with salt and pepper.

Right before you plate the cauliflower, toss in parsley and mix well.

Haricots Verts and Tomato

Serves 4-6

1 pound haricots verts, cut in half

2 cups red pearl onions, cleaned

Olive oil as needed, about ¾ cup

Salt and pepper

10 plum tomatoes, cut in half and oven-dried

3 tablespoons sugar

7 sprigs thyme, picked

1 cup tomato sauce or marinara

Blanch haricots verts in boiling salted water, cool in an ice bath, and hold until needed.

Preheat oven to 375°F. Put cleaned pearl onions in a small bowl and lightly coat them with olive oil, salt, and pepper. Place in a pan or on baking sheet in oven for 15 to 20 minutes, until they are roasted through and tender. Remove and hold until needed.

Turn down oven to 200°F. Cut tomatoes in half from top to bottom and lay on a baking sheet with cut side up. Lightly coat with olive oil, salt, and pepper. Cover tops of all tomatoes with sugar and picked thyme. Bake tomatoes in oven for 3 hours. They will become dark, but that's okay!

To assemble, lightly coat a large sauté pan with oil over medium-high heat and add onions and haricots verts. Cook for 2 to 3 minutes and then add oven-dried tomatoes and marinara sauce. Taste for seasoning, and adjust with salt and pepper. Plate in a suitable bowl and enjoy!

Scotto Polenta

Serves 5-7

1 quart heavy cream

1 quart milk

2 cups polenta

8 ounces mascarpone

Salt, to taste

Put cream and milk into a pot over medium-high heat and, stirring regularly, bring mixture up to a steam. When liquid is hot, pour in polenta, stirring the entire time, until polenta has been cooked through.

Once it has been thoroughly cooked, remove from heat and fold in mascarpone. Adjust seasoning with salt.

Mama Scotto's Sausage and Rice Stuffing

Fills one 18- to 20-pound turkey

¼ cup extra-virgin olive oil, plus more for finishing

1 pound Italian sausage without casing (ground or loose sausage)

1 large onion, diced large

1 pound ground beef

1 pound ground veal

2 pounds rice, uncooked

1½ pounds mozzarella cheese, sliced

½ cup Parmesan cheese, grated

Preheat oven to 350°F. In a large saucepan over medium-high heat, warm 2 tablespoons of extra-virgin olive oil and add sausage and cook until it is brown. Remove it to a large bowl. In remaining 2 tablespoons of olive oil, sauté onion, beef, and veal until brown and add mixture to bowl of sausage.

Cook rice according to directions on package. In a large bowl, stir rice, mozzarella, and Parmesan together with meat mixture.

Place mixture in a casserole dish and bake for 20 minutes, or until cheese is melted. Remove from oven, drizzle with extra-virgin olive oil, and serve immediately.

Chef's Trick! Add a little extra Parmesan for the last 5 to 10 minutes of baking for a nice crust on top—it's always a crowd pleaser.

CANNOLI • **201**

BOMBOLONI WITH CHOCOLATE AND CARAMEL SAUCES • **202**

CHOCOLATE PANNA COTTA • **204**

CREAMY RICOTTA CHEESECAKE • **206**

CHOCOLATE MASCARPONE CREAM PIE • **208**

RICOTTA FRITTERS • **209**

PUMPKIN CHOCOLATE TIRAMISU • **210**

Desserts

Cannoli

Serves 6–8

2 cups cannoli cream

1½ cups confectioners' sugar, plus more to garnish

2 tablespoons vanilla extract

2 cups miniature chocolate chips

12 medium to small cannoli shells

Cocoa powder, to garnish

Combine all ingredients, except cannoli shells and garnishes, and mix well. Put mixture in a disposable piping bag and then pipe it into cannoli shells. Put a small touch of cannoli cream underneath each cannoli shell to hold it in place as you pipe.

Garnish with confectioners' sugar and cocoa powder.

Bomboloni with Chocolate and Caramel Sauces

Serves 10 or more

1 pound white superfine sugar

2 pounds cornstarch

2 tablespoons baking powder

3 pounds ricotta

12 eggs

2 tablespoons vanilla puree

Mix dry ingredients together very well in a mixer. Slowly mix in wet ingredients until a batter is formed. It should be fairly thick.

Preheat fryer to 375°F. Fry scoops of batter for at least 8 to 10 minutes. (Having a basket on top helps bomboloni brown uniformly and cook evenly, but doesn't really speed up the process.)

Serve with Chocolate and Caramel Sauces.

Bomboloni with Chocolate and Caramel Sauces, cont.

CHOCOLATE SAUCE

1 pound dark chocolate

2 pounds pâté à glacer

½ cup blended oil

Heat chocolate in a double boiler and incorporate pâté à glacer and oil. Mix well and hold hot.

If you don't have pâté à glacer, it's okay—just don't add oil! You can also use store-bought chocolate sauce.

CARAMEL SAUCE

1 cup granulated sugar

¼ cup water

6 tablespoons unsalted butter, cut into pieces

½ cup heavy cream

1 teaspoon vanilla extract

Pinch of salt

Add sugar and water to a 3-quart heavy-bottomed saucepan; stir a little so it sits in a flat, even layer. Warm pan over medium heat and cook until sugar dissolves, turns clear, and starts to bubble. (It will be cloudy at first, but will turn into a clear, bubbling liquid.) This takes 3 to 4 minutes. At this point, do not stir again— simply allow mixture to bubble, swirl saucepan occasionally, and brush down sides of pan as needed to prevent crystallization.

Sugar will form clumps, but continue swirling and cooking for another 8 to 12 minutes, until mixture thickens and turns a deep amber color, like honey. Keep a watchful eye so the mixture doesn't burn.

Carefully add butter and whisk until completely melted. (The caramel will bubble up rapidly, so be careful and continue to whisk.) Remove saucepan from heat and slowly pour in cream, whisking continuously until all of cream has been incorporated.

Whisk in vanilla and salt and set aside to cool in pan for 10 minutes. Then pour into a glass vessel and allow to cool completely.

Chocolate Panna Cotta

Serves 4–6

7 sheets gelatin

Ice water

1½ cups milk

3 cups heavy cream

1 cup sugar

1 vanilla bean, cleaned well

8 ounces dark chocolate, chopped

Allow sheets of gelatin to sit in ice water for about 2 minutes, until very soft and spongy. Squeeze out as much water as possible.

Add milk, cream, sugar, vanilla bean, and chocolate to a small saucepan and bring to a simmer, continually stirring until all ingredients are combined well and chocolate has melted entirely. Remove liquid from heat. Squeeze gelatin *very well* and stir into liquid. Pour mixture into desired vessels (container, cups, molds, and so on).

Serve with fresh fruits, whipped cream, or toasted nuts.

Creamy Ricotta Cheesecake

Serves 12

GRAHAM CRACKER CRUST

1 cup graham cracker crumbs

¼ cup all-purpose flour

3 tablespoons sugar

½ cup butter, melted

RICOTTA FILLING

1 pound cream cheese

1½ pounds whole-milk ricotta cheese (preferably fresh—available in Italian markets and specialty food stores)

6 eggs

1¼ cups sugar

1 tablespoon vanilla extract

To make graham cracker crust: Preheat oven to 350°F. Line bottom of a 10-inch springform pan with baking parchment or waxed paper. Tightly cover outside of pan with foil (it has to be watertight). In a medium bowl, mix all ingredients until blended. Press crumb mixture into the springform pan evenly, covering the bottom. Bake for 15 minutes, or until golden brown. Remove from oven and reduce heat to 325°F.

To make ricotta filling: In a food processor or blender, puree two cheeses together until smooth. Transfer to a mixing bowl; add eggs, sugar, and vanilla, and whisk until well blended. Pour mixture into graham cracker crust and place springform pan into a larger pan. Pour enough water into larger pan to reach halfway up the sides of the springform pan. Bake for 2 hours. At the end of this time, shut off oven, open oven door slightly, and allow cheesecake to cool in oven for at least an hour. Then remove from oven and let cool to room temperature. Refrigerate at least overnight.

To remove cheesecake from springform pan, run a hot, wet knife around edge of cake and remove collar of pan. Invert cake onto a plate and remove springform bottom and parchment paper. Flip cake back onto a serving plate and cut with a hot, wet knife.

Serve with fresh berries.

Chocolate Mascarpone Cream Pie

Serves 8

GRAHAM CRACKER CRUST

1½ cups graham cracker crumbs

½ cup sugar

½ cup all-purpose flour

1½ cups butter, melted

CHOCOLATE FILLING

1 cup sugar

¼ cup cornstarch

¼ teaspoon salt

3 cups whole milk

3 egg yolks, slightly beaten

2 tablespoons butter

2 teaspoons vanilla extract

¼ cup unsweetened chocolate, finely chopped

WHIPPED TOPPING

2 cups mascarpone

2 cups heavy cream

¼ cup sugar

1 teaspoon vanilla extract

To make graham cracker crust: Preheat oven to 350°F. Grease a 9-inch pie pan with 2 tablespoons of butter or nonstick spray. In a medium bowl, mix ingredients for graham cracker crust together until blended. Press into bottom and sides of pie pan to a thickness of about one-quarter inch (you'll have some left over). Bake for 12 minutes, or until golden brown. Let cool.

To make chocolate filling: In a medium saucepan, combine sugar, cornstarch, and salt. Stir in milk, blending well. Cook over medium heat, stirring constantly, until mixture boils and thickens, about 2 minutes. Remove from heat. Blend a small amount of hot mixture into egg yolks to temper them. Pour egg yolks into saucepan, blending thoroughly.

Heat mixture over high heat, stirring constantly, until it just begins to bubble, about 3 minutes. Remove from heat and stir in butter, vanilla, and chocolate. Stir until chocolate melts completely. Pour the mixture into baked pie shell and refrigerate, uncovered, for at least 1 hour.

To make whipped topping: In a large bowl, combine all topping ingredients and whip until stiff. Spread over chocolate filling and return pie to refrigerator for at least 2 more hours.

Ricotta Fritters

Yields 25–30 fritters (a snack for 6–8)

4 eggs

¼ cup sugar

1 pound ricotta cheese

½ teaspoon vanilla extract

½ cup all-purpose flour

½ cup cake flour

1 tablespoon baking powder

1 pinch salt

Oil, for frying

Powdered sugar, to garnish

Small jar of chestnut honey, to garnish

Mix eggs and sugar together and then stir in ricotta and vanilla.

In a separate bowl, sift together all-purpose flour, cake flour, baking powder, and salt. Add to egg mixture and beat until smooth. Allow mixture to rest and cool in refrigerator. (The colder the batter is, the more uniform the pieces will be.)

Fill a pot or deep-fryer half full with oil. Heat oil to 350°F (oil expands when hot, so start with less, and then add as needed).

Drop dough into hot oil by the tablespoonful. Fry until golden brown, straining out with a high-temperature slotted spoon.

Remove fritters from oil and drain on a paper towel. Dust with powdered sugar, drizzle with warm chestnut honey, and serve immediately.

Chef's Trick! Dip the spoon in the fryer oil before spooning batter to help the batter not stick on the spoon.

Pumpkin Chocolate Tiramisu

Serves 12

- 4 egg yolks
- 1¼ cups sugar
- 2 cups pumpkin puree
- 2 cups mascarpone
- 1½ cups heavy cream
- 4 sheets gelatin
- ¼ cup brandy
- 2 cups espresso
- 1 layer of a 10-inch chocolate cake

In bowl of an electric mixer, whip egg yolks on high speed with ¾ cup sugar until mixture is pale yellow and has tripled in volume. Add pumpkin and mascarpone and whip again until light, about 2 minutes on high speed. Transfer pumpkin mixture to a large mixing bowl.

Put cream and ¼ cup sugar into bowl of electric mixer. Whip cream until stiff peaks form and then fold it into pumpkin mixture.

Soak gelatin sheets in cold water. Remove from water and squeeze out excess water. Cover with brandy in a small saucepan and heat over a low flame, just until gelatin melts.

Fold a small amount of pumpkin-cream mixture into gelatin to temper it. Then mix all gelatin into cream.

Dissolve remaining ¼ cup sugar in espresso. Divide cake layer in half horizontally and place one layer on a serving plate. Soak that layer with half of espresso.

Pour half of cream mixture on top of espresso-soaked cake layer. Place second cake layer on top of cream. Soak that layer with remaining espresso and top it with remaining cream. Wrap in plastic wrap and refrigerate at least overnight.

Cocktails

POMEGRANATE TEQUILA COCKTAIL • **212**

WATERMELON BLISS • **212**

FROSÉ WITH FRESH RASPBERRIES • **213**

THE PALOMA • **214**

MAPLE MARGARITA • **215**

HOLIDAY SOUR • **215**

MELONE MARGARITA • **216**

LA RESISTENZA • **217**

DRESS THE EMPRESS • **217**

Pomegranate Tequila Cocktail

Serves 4–6

6 shots tequila

4 cups ice cubes or crushed ice

⅔ cup plus 1 tablespoon pomegranate juice

4 cups soda water

GARNISHES

1 sprig fresh mint (per glass)

1 sliced lime (per glass)

1 handful fresh pomegranate seeds

Measure tequila and pour it into a cocktail shaker. Add ice cubes and pomegranate juice and shake.

Pour drinks into 4 to 6 glasses and top up with soda water. Add mint, lime, and fresh pomegranate rubies to each glass and serve.

Watermelon Bliss

Serves 6

6 ounces Ketel One Botanical Cucumber & Mint vodka

4½ ounces watermelon juice

1 bottle Prosecco

Sliced watermelon, for garnish

For each serving, add 1 ounce of vodka to a champagne flute. Add ¾ ounce watermelon juice. Pour Prosecco to top of flute.

Garnish with a piece of watermelon and enjoy!

Frosé with Fresh Raspberries

Serves 4–6

1 750-ml bottle bold rosé

½ cup sugar

½ cup water

8 ounces raspberries

2½ ounces fresh lemon juice

1 cup crushed ice

Pour rosé into a 13 × 9-inch pan and freeze until almost solid, at least 6 hours (it won't completely solidify because of the alcohol).

When rosé is ready, bring sugar and water to a boil in a medium saucepan; cook, stirring constantly, until sugar dissolves, about 3 minutes. Add raspberries, remove from heat, and let sit for 30 minutes; cover and chill until cold, another 30 minutes.

Scrape rosé into a blender. Add raspberries, lemon juice, and crushed ice and puree until smooth. Transfer blender jar to freezer and freeze until frosé is thickened, about 25–35 minutes.

Blend again until frosé is slushy. Divide among glasses.

Chef's Trick! *Did you know . . .* Rosé can be frozen 1 week ahead of time.

The Paloma

This is a classic cocktail, easy to make, and very refreshing.

Serves 6

7½ ounces tequila

2½ ounces fresh lime juice

2 ounces agave nectar (optional)

6 ounces fresh grapefruit juice

Soda water

GARNISHES

Rosemary sprig

Grapefruit wedge

Lime wedge

Combine tequila and fresh lime juice in a cocktail shaker with ice. Feel free to add agave nectar to sweeten the drink! Shake well and strain into a glass with ice. Top off with grapefruit juice and soda water.

Garnish each glass with a rosemary sprig and wedges of grapefruit and lime.

Maple Margarita

Serves 6

12 ounces mezcal

1½ ounces triple sec

9 ounces lime juice

Maple syrup

For each serving, pour 2 ounces of mezcal into a shaker with ice. Add ¼ ounce of triple sec and 1½–2 ounces lime juice. Shake well for 15 seconds and pour mixture into a glass.

Drizzle with maple syrup. Stir and enjoy!

Holiday Sour

For 1 serving

¾ ounce lemon juice

¾ ounce cranberry syrup

1½ ounces green apple soaked bourbon

½ ounce Campari

1 egg white

Dry shake ingredients (without ice) very well for 15 seconds. Add ice and shake until well chilled. Double strain and serve.

For 6 servings

4½ ounces lemon juice

4½ ounces cranberry syrup

9 ounces green apple soaked bourbon

3 ounces Campari

6 egg whites

Melone Margarita

Serves 1

2 ounces tequila

1 ounce melon liqueur

1 ounce lime juice

1½ ounces triple sec

Splash of sour mix

Shake and serve!

La Resistenza

Serves 1

¼ ounce lime juice

Tajin (or other spicy bitters)

2 ounces Gran Coramino Cristalino Reposado tequila

¾ ounce Pom-Infused Clase Azul tequila

½ ounce Campari

½ ounce pineapple juice

Dehydrated lemon slice, for garnish

Prep glass by lining rim with lime juice and lightly pressing rim in Tajin (we recommend using a small plate you can pour the Tajin into!).

Grab a shaker, fill it with ice, and add all ingredients. Lightly shake with ice intact and pour into a glass. Finish with a dehydrated lemon slice.

Dress the Empress

Serves 1

½ ounce melon liqueur

2 ounces pineapple juice

1 ounce Aperol

¼ ounce lime juice

¼ ounce Empress gin

Pour melon liqueur into bottom of glass. In a shaker, combine pineapple juice, Aperol, and lime juice. Gently pour mixture on top of melon layer, leaving some room to top it off with Empress gin.

< Melone Margarita, La Resistenza, and Dress the Empress.

Sample Menus

Holiday Menu

Baked Clams

Eggplant and Zucchini Pie

Tagliolini with Crab Ragù

Zuppa di Pesce

Rack of Lamb with Cannellini Bean Salad
 and Lemon-Caper Salsa Verde

Mama Scotto's Sausage and Rice Stuffing

Scotto Polenta

Cannoli

Creamy Ricotta Cheesecake

Holiday Sour

Party Menu

Lobster Arancini

Goat Cheese and Prosciutto Pinwheels

Prosciutto-Wrapped Asparagus with Parmesan Cheese

Mom's Stuffed Mushrooms

Cannellini Bean Dip

Chickpea alla Fresco Dip

Cod Puree Dip

Ricotta with Lemon Zest Dip

Shrimp with Watermelon and Tomato Salad

Ricotta Fritters

Date Night Menu

Elaina's Tomato Bruschetta

Summer Salad with Raspberry Vinaigrette

Sunday Sauce with Meatballs, Sausages, and Pork Chops

Prime Rib with Roasted Potatoes and Mushrooms

Bomboloni with Chocolate and Caramel Sauces

Chocolate Panna Cotta

Scotto Sisters' Tips

Here we offer some general kitchen tips for working in the kitchen along with our recommendations for the Essential Pantry and Must-Have Utensils. Also be on the lookout for our Chef's Tricks, which are specific to individual recipes.

Take your time. Read the whole recipe before you begin and take this opportunity to ensure you have all the needed ingredients. Rushing through a recipe increases your chances of messing things up—like skipping a step or using the wrong measurement.

Rely on your senses. As you cook, use your senses—not just the recipe—for smell, color, texture, and taste. And always taste as you go.

Use a wooden spoon to mix ingredients.
A wooden spoon is softer and can mix better than a metal or plastic spoon. It also doesn't conduct heat, which means you can use it to stir sauces without the spoon getting hot too quickly. Just make sure to maintain your spoons so no little chips of wood fall into the food.

Keep your cooking knives sharpened.
A dull knife is more dangerous than a sharp knife.

Cooking with oil. Always gently heat the oil and use a thermometer (there is no trick for that one—always choose the side of safety first!). In a sauté pan, the oil will ripple like water when you move the pan back and forth and side to side. When it reaches about 280–320°F or so, or comes to a light smoke, that's a good time to start adding ingredients.

Olive oil. Invest in high-quality extra-virgin olive oil for special meals or to drizzle over dishes to accent flavors.

Salt and pepper. Always add to taste and/or dietary needs. Remember you can always add!

Salting water for pasta and vegetables. You should be able to taste the salt, *but* it should not be salty!

Blanching vegetables. The pot of water should be boiling *well* before adding vegetables! Always have an ice bath and suitable utensils for straining and/or draining.

Boiling potatoes. Always bring the potatoes up from cold to simmer with the potatoes *inside* the water from the start, which allows them to cook evenly. Always check for salt.

Cooking meats. Always allow the protein to sit out for at least an hour or so to come to room temperature. This step allows for even cooking and, in some cases, faster cooking. The protein may sweat a little bit after coming to room temperature—make sure to pat it dry.

THE ESSENTIAL PANTRY

White refined sugar
Kosher salt
White all-purpose flour
Extra-virgin olive oil
Blended vegetable oil (canola oil)
Red wine vinegar
Balsamic vinegar
Pepper mill (pre-ground pepper can work)
Ground white pepper
Dry herbs (thyme, parsley, oregano, bay leaf)
Onion powder
Garlic powder
Chili flakes
Grated Parmesan cheese (refrigerator)
Canned plum tomatoes
Canned crushed tomatoes
Tomato paste
Chicken, beef, fish, and vegetable broths
Ketchup
Hot sauce (Tabasco)
Canned or dry beans
Rice
Dry pasta
Gelatin sheets

MUST-HAVE UTENSILS

Silicone high-temperature spatula
Metal fish spatula
Whisk
Kitchen towels or kitchen mittens or hot pads
Clean cutting board
Sharp knives (sharp knives are actually safer knives)
Carving knife
Meat fork
Meat thermometer
High-temperature metal pans (nonstick is okay)
Oven-safe baking dishes (casseroles, baking trays, etc.)
Measuring cups
Measuring spoons
Food processor
Kitchen scale
Rolling pin (a wine bottle can also work)
Pasta machine
Strainer (colander)
Peeler
Meat tenderizer
Kitchen shears
Nesting mixing bowls
Tongs
Microplane (cheese grater)

Fish. Never over-season seafood. You want to be able to still taste the flavor of the fish. Simply use lemon juice and salt and pepper. Seafood should never smell fishy—that's a sure sign that it's starting to go bad. It should smell like the ocean!

Let chicken soak in buttermilk for 48 hours. Chicken tends to dry out when cooking. This classic Old-World tip results in succulent chicken. The buttermilk helps to both tenderize and add moisture to the chicken.

Brown your meat. If you're cooking beef or lamb, before you put it in the oven at the desired temperature, brown it off in a frying pan to add texture and great flavor. Sealing flavor in is an old wives' tale!

Long, low, and slow. When you're cooking a casserole or a stew in one pot, so long as there's enough liquid, the longer you cook it at a lower temperature, the better it's going to taste.

When making homemade pasta. Mixing the pasta dough in a large bowl saves the mess on the counter. Once the pasta is kneaded, cover the bowl with plastic wrap and allow it to rest for about 30 minutes at room temperature before you roll it out and portion into desired pieces.

Things that grow together go together. Fruits and vegetables that ripen at the same time of year often taste great together. For example, peppers mixed with tomatoes, squash and sweet corn, and kale and pumpkin are all great combinations.

Peel tomatoes easily. Cut an X on the bottom of a tomato and then drop it into a pot of boiling water for 15 to 30 seconds. Cool it down in an ice bath and the skin should peel right off.

No luck finding shallots? Replace shallots with a combination of onions and garlic.

Can't find a Meyer lemon? Substitute half a lemon and half an orange as a replacement for a Meyer lemon.

Storing garlic. To keep whole garlic from going rancid, always store it at room temperature. Peeled garlic goes in the fridge!

Sautéing garlic. Use sliced garlic instead of minced to prevent burning.

After handling garlic. Rub your fingers on stainless steel, such as your sink, to get rid of the odor.

Acknowledgments
OUR FRESCO FAMILY

It has been quite the journey for Fresco by Scotto and Fresco on the Go. We've learned that it takes a village to accomplish each task to make our restaurant a remarkable place, so we need to make sure we take the time to thank all the amazing people who have helped us move forward.

First and foremost, we would like to thank Manny Carabel, Michael Simon, Eric Striffler, Yorgos Fasoulis, and Ellen Wolff—all the great photographers who helped make this cookbook come visually alive and showcased the excitement of the new Fresco. We would also like to thank the team that gathered the amazing photos of our food and the fantastic cover photo: Hudi Greenberger, Justin Jagiello, Janine Kalesis, and Penelope Bouklas.

We thank Jaret Keller and Tara Halper, our amazing PR machine. They have helped us through the past decade with the restaurant. Through their guidance and creativity, we've been able to create a national brand for Fresco by Scotto.

Next, we are grateful to our friends in the media who have posted and shared our story, including the *Good Day New York* crew: Bianca Peters, Mike Woods, and Ines Rosales. Also, we thank Rosanna's bosses at Fox 5: Lew Leone, Byron Harmon, Jack Abernethy, Emad Asghar, and Lamar Goering.

In addition, we'd like to give a special thank-you to Kelly Ripa and Mark Consuelos, Hoda Kotb, Al Roker, Wendy Williams, Sara Gore, Luann De Lesseps, Melissa and Joe Gorga, Jill Martin, Elvis Duran, Foodgod, Lil "Mo" Mozzarella, Meals by Cug, and Lee Schrager.

We thank P.J. Tierney for all of her amazing work in putting together this fantastic cookbook. It takes someone with a lot of energy to deal with all the different personalities in the Scotto family, so we are grateful for her passion in bringing this book to life in a such short time!

We would also like to thank our executive chef, Benjamin Kacmarcik. Ben has a great demeanor and presence in the kitchen. He's calm, composed, and works incredibly hard to bring a new flare to the Fresco menu. He's taken many of our old staples, like breadsticks or chips, and transformed them into something unique and tasty. His specials are to die for, and the new scrumptious desserts he creates are out of this world. He took a lot of time out of his schedule to help break down each of the recipes in this book. It takes a lot of patience to bring our kitchen at the restaurant to yours in your home. We also can't forget the second-in-command, our sous chef Luis Orlando Alvarez, who prepared all the dishes for the amazing food shots placed throughout this book. He's been serving up delicious meals at our restaurant since 1998!

Fresco wouldn't be as amazing as it is now without the diligent and gracious effort that our staff gives. From the servers to the cooks in the kitchen, everyone has really come together to make Fresco an incredibly fun environment for eating and working. Some of these servers have been working for us for all of our operating years, giving their all to make Fresco run smoothly and properly—and doing so with a smile on their face. The following staff have weathered the storm with us for more than nine years: Pedro Flores Ramirez, Carlos Blanco, Pedro Martinez, Luis Ortega, Klever Dutan-Quito, Wilson Ortiz, and Estadislao Ramirez.

During this new phase of our business, our staff has been more than willing to help make Fresco the exciting destination it has become. They are more than happy to partake in each new idea we come up with. The dessert parades we have usually involve a dozen or so of our employees, and they are pleased to assist in these demonstrations. Later in the night, we turn up our new theme song, "Bella Ciao," and almost all our servers are willing to dance in between the tables. They do so with such enthusiasm that it makes it even more enticing for our customers to partake.

We cannot thank our remarkable team enough for the time and energy they dedicate. We'd especially like to give a shout-out to our managers Ciprian Nourescu, Marco Barrera, Rita Papa, and Will Baltodano—and Lori Jakubowski, our bookkeeper extraordinaire—for their undying effort and participation throughout the restaurant's rebirth. Let's not forget to mention our party captain, Dennis Ryan, one of our original employees, who has been with us through thick and thin. We want to applaud the smiling faces we see upon entering Fresco: Matilda Isabella, Kamara Graves, Michelle Ewell, and Agnesa Maliqi.

Outside the restaurant, we would like to thank Hugo Rafael Fermin and the rest of the security staff. They've spent many nights outside making sure our diners are enjoying themselves in a safe environment.

And we can't forget to mention those who work next door to Fresco. Our On the Go family has been with us for the past twenty-three years, making sure that the fast-casual side of our business runs as smoothly as possible. Victor Quizhpi, Nataly Herrera, Galo Lopez, and Luis Sanaicela have been with us from the beginning. Their hard work and passion have made Fresco on the Go a major success not only as a lunch destination but also as a focal point for our catering business for offices and concerts. In addition, Miguel Limon Munoz, Albert Cruz, and Julio Hernandez have all worked at On the Go for the past ten years, bringing their all to the business.

We would like to thank our loyal Scotto Sisters community. They have been with us through the entire process of the reconstruction and some of our toughest times of the year. Their support has been unquestionable and amazing. Any endeavor we decide to undergo, they are willing and supportive without question. They have our backs through thick and thin.

Last but not least, we especially want to thank our two children Dan Faucetta and Jenna Ruggiero. They were asked to help us with this project and took the reins, putting in tireless effort to bring this cookbook to life. They were so diligent and hard-working that it allowed us to continue our day jobs without having to worry. It's been such a blessing to work alongside our children and it has made us incredibly proud watching them turn this idea into a physical book for your enjoyment.

To all of our loyal customers at Fresco by Scotto, we thank you for supporting us throughout these beautiful thirty years. And, of course, love and appreciation to our wonderful families, who lifted us during the trying times and partied with us in the rebirth of Fresco. Here's to us!

Index

Photos are indicated by **_bold italic_** page numbers.

Adams, Eric, 63, 74, 75

Amatriciana, 149

anchovies: Puttanesca Salsa Verde, 182, **_183_**

Aniston, Jennifer, 26, **_26_**

Aperol: Dress the Empress, 217

arugula: Arugula and Red Onion Salad, 176; Balsamic Skirt Steak with Sun-Dried Tomato Pesto and Arugula Salad, 172–73; Citrus Fregula Salad, 188–89; Grilled Angus Sirloin Steak Pizzaiola with Simple Arugula Salad, **_168_**, 169–70; Pan-Seared Salmon with Shaved Fennel and Arugula Salad, 186; Quinoa Arugula Salad with Citrus Vinaigrette, 192; Veal Milanese, 166, **_167_**

asparagus: Cannellini Bean Salad, 162–63; Larry's Lemon Capellini Primavera, **_133_**, 134–35; Prosciutto-Wrapped Asparagus with Parmesan Cheese, 108

Baio, Scott, **_9_**

Baked Clams, 179

Baked Ricotta Dip with Crostini, 102, **_103_**

balsamic vinegar and glaze: balsamic glaze alternative, 124; Elaina's Tomato Bruschetta, **_104_**, 105; Shrimp with Watermelon and Tomato Salad, 124, **_125_**; steak marinade, 172

basil, 118, 131; Citrus Fregula Salad, 188–89; Garganelli with Broccoli Rabe and Sausage, 148; Grilled Pizza Margherita, 98–99; Pesto, 137; Pesto Genovese, 150–51; Pizzaiola Sauce, 170; Rigatoni with Short-Rib Ragù, 144–45; Rosanna's Spaghetti alla Nerano, 136; Tagliolini with Crab Ragù, **_140_**, 141–42; Tomato Sauce, 143

beef: Fresco Burger, **_158_**, 159–60; Fresco by Scotto's Signature Meatballs, 161; Mama Scotto's Sausage and Rice Stuffing, 198; Pasta Bolognese, 138. *See also* ribs

beef stock: Braised Short Ribs, 174

beets: Beet Salad with Toasted Pistachios and Citrus Vinaigrette, 126

bell peppers: Goat Cheese and Prosciutto Pinwheels, 106; Seafood Stew or "Cioppino," 121

Bel Paese cheese: Fresco by Scotto's Signature Meatballs, 161; Grilled Pizza Margherita, 98–99

bitters, spicy, 217

Bomboloni with Chocolate and Caramel Sauces, **_202_**, 202–3

bourbon, 215

Braised Lamb Shanks, 171

Braised Short Ribs with Roasted Garlic Mashed Potatoes, 174–75

brandy, 209

branzino: Grilled Branzino, 182, **_183_**

bread, 187; Baked Ricotta Dip with Crostini, 102, **_103_**; Elaina's Tomato Bruschetta, **_104_**, 105; Panzanella Salad, 187

bread crumbs: Baked Clams, 179; Eggplant and Zucchini Pie, 100–101; Fresco by Scotto's Signature Meatballs, 161; Lemon Gremolata, 135; Lobster Arancini, **_184_**, 185; Mini Lentil

Burgers, 107; Mom's Stuffed Mushrooms, 109; Tomato-and-Herb-Crusted Filet of Sole, 178; Veal Milanese, 166–67, **167**

broccoli: Penne Pasta Primavera, 131

broccoli rabe: Garganelli with Broccoli Rabe and Sausage, 148

Brooklyn family home, 1, 2, 7, 15, **17**

bruschetta: Elaina's Tomato Bruschetta, 105

burgers: Fresco Burger, **158**, 159–60; Mini Lentil Burgers, 107

butter: Ravioli with Brown Butter Sage Sauce, 139

buttermilk, chicken soaked in, 222

butternut squash: Panzanella Salad, 187

Cabo San Lucas, Mexico, 53–54

calachote, 19

calamari: Fritto Misto, **114**, 115; Marinated Seafood Salad, 180; Risotto with Lobster, Shrimp, and Calamari, 152–53; Seafood Stew or "Cioppino," **120**, 121

Campari: Holiday Sour, 215; La Resistenza, 217

cannellini beans: Cannellini Bean Dip, 112; Cannellini Bean Salad, 162–63; Zuppa di Pesce, 118

cannoli: Cannoli (dessert), **200**, 201; Golden, at Fresco, **41**, 45, **45**, **78**, 79, **79**

capellini, **133**; Capellini with Mushroom Ragù, 132, **133**; Larry's Lemon Capellini Primavera, **133**, 134–35

Capellini with Mushroom Ragù, 132, **133**

capers: Lemon-Caper Salsa Verde, 162–63; Pan-Seared Dover Sole with Sautéed Spinach, 181; Pizzaiola Sauce, 170; Puttanesca Salsa Verde, 182, **183**

Caprese Salad, **20**

Capri, Italy, 4, 33

Caramel Sauce, **202**, 202–3

Castelvetrano olives: Pizzaiola Sauce, 170; Puttanesca Salsa Verde, 182, **183**

cauliflower: Cauliflower and Roasted Garlic, 195; Cauliflower Puree, 188–89

celebrities: on Fresco photo wall, 55, **58**, 59–60, **61–62**, **63**, 63–65, **64**; at Fresco reopening night, **70**, 71, **73**, 73–74. *See also specific celebrities*

champagne vinegar, 126, 160, 189

Cheban, Jonathan (Foodgod), 44–45, **45**

cheese. *See specific cheeses*

Chef's Tricks and Tips: baked Parmesan topper, 198; breading, 100, 166; burger buns, 159; crab preparation, 142; forming meatballs, 161; freezing rosé, 213; heating oil and deep frying, 208, 220; leftovers, 148; lemon oil, 134; lobster, 152; mushrooms, 109, 132; pantry essentials, 221; pasta dough, 130, 223; peeling tomatoes, 223; pesto, 137; pickling, 160; utensils, 220, 222

Chenoweth, Kristin, **64**

chestnut honey: Ricotta Fritters, 209

chicken: buttermilk-soaked, 222; Chicken Cotoletta, 176; Pasta Bolognese, 138; Roasted Half Chicken, 164

chicken stock: Braised Lamb Shanks, 171; Risotto with Lobster, Shrimp, and Calamari, 152–53

Chickpea alla Fresco Dip, 110, **111**

chocolate: Chocolate Sauce, **202**, 202–3; Chocolate Mascarpone Cream Pie, 208; Chocolate Panna Cotta, 204, **205**; Pumpkin Chocolate Tiramisu, 210

chocolate chips: Cannoli, **200**, 201

Cioppino, **120**, 121

Citrus Fregula Salad, 188–89

Citrus Vinaigrette, 192; Beet Salad with, 126; Shaved Fennel and Arugula Salad with, 186; Quinoa Arugula Salad with, 192

clams: Baked Clams, 179; Seafood Stew, **120**, 121; Zuppa di Pesce, 118

Clarity (Faucetta, D.), 93

Clinton, Bill, 63, 75, **80**, 81–83, **82**

Clinton, Hillary, **11**, 63, 75, **80**, 81–83

Clooney, George, 54, 55

cocktails: family tradition and, 17, 19; recipes, 212–17

Cod Puree Dip, 110, **111**

Consuelos, Mark, 71

cookbooks, previous, 27, 51, 55, **57**, 93

cooking tips. *See Chef's Tricks and Tips*

Countess Luann, 89, **89**

Couric, Katie, **56**

COVID pandemic: Fresco and, 25, 28, 30–31, 35–36, 67, 68, 74; Instagram following during, 39; and origins of Scotto Sisters Schmoozing, 28, 39; QVC partnership and, 47; Sunday Suppers and, 23

crab: crab stock, 142; Marinated Seafood Salad, 180; Tagliolini with Crab Ragù, **140**, 141–42

cranberry syrup: Holiday Sour, 215

cream: Caramel Sauce, **202**, 202–3; Cauliflower Puree, 188–89; Chocolate Mascarpone Cream Pie, 208; Chocolate Panna Cotta, 204, **205**; Cod Puree Dip, 110, **111**; Mashed Potatoes, 164; Parmesan-Crusted Mashed Potatoes, 193; Roasted Garlic Mashed Potatoes, 174–75; Scotto Polenta, 197

cream cheese: Creamy Ricotta Cheesecake, 206, **207**

Creamy Ricotta Cheesecake, 206, **207**

croutons, 187

cucumbers: pickles, homemade, 160; Shrimp with Watermelon and Tomato Salad, 124, **125**; Summer Salad with Raspberry Vinaigrette, 122–23

Cugine, 43–44, **44**

Dad. *See* Scotto, Anthony, Sr.

Danny (Elaina's son). *See* Faucetta, Danny

date night sample menu, 219

DeGeneres, Ellen, 27, 55, 57, **57**, 64

doughs: gnocchi, 146; pasta, 130, 223; pizza, 98–99, 116

Drasler, Greg, 25; art by, 37

dressings, salad: Citrus Vinaigrette, 192; Raspberry or Red Wine Vinaigrette, 123

Dress the Empress, 217

Duran, Elvis, 71, 74

Eggplant and Zucchini Pie, 100–101

eggs: Bomboloni, **202**, 202–3; Chocolate Mascarpone Cream Pie, 208; Creamy Ricotta Cheesecake, 206, **207**; Eggplant and Zucchini Pie, 100–101; Holiday Sour, 215; Pizza Rustica, 116; Ricotta Fritters, 209; Veal Milanese, 166–67, **167**

Elaina's Tomato Bruschetta, **104**, 105

Ellen DeGeneres Show, The, 27, 55, 57, 64

espresso: Pumpkin Chocolate Tiramisu, 210

family: Brooklyn home and history for, 1, 2, 7, 15, **17**; *Family Circle* photo of, 65, **65**; generations at Fresco, 9, 12, 27, **90**, 91–93, **92**, **93**; impact of pandemic on, 28; importance of, 3, 7; Italy and, 4–5, 33, 54–55, **55**; traditions, 15–23. *See also specific family members*

Family Circle (magazine), 65, **65**

farfalle, 130

Faucetta, Danny, 4, **4**, 5, **5**, 21, 54, 92–93, **93**

Faucetta, Julia, 4, **5**, 21, **50**, 92, **93**

fava beans: Quinoa Arugula Salad, 192

fennel bulb: Braised Short Ribs, 174–75; Garganelli with Broccoli Rabe and Sausage, 148; Pasta Bolognese, 138; Shaved Fennel and Arugula Salad, 186

fettucine, 130

fish. *See specific types of fish*

Foodgod (Jonathan Cheban), 44–45, **45**

food influencers, **43**, 43–45. *See also* Scotto Sisters Schmoozing

Fox 5, 2, 25, 53, **53**, 65

fregula: Citrus Fregula Salad, 188–89

Fresco Burger, **158**, 159–60

Fresco by Scotto (Fresco): accolades and fame for, 13, 25–27; beginnings, 8–9, 25–26, 67; "Bella Ciao" song and dance at, 33–35, **35**; Christmas Eve celebration at, 2; Bill Clinton at, 63, **80**, 81–83, **82**; COVID pandemic and, 25, 28, 30–31, 35–36, 67, 68, 74; Danny working at, 4, 5, 92–93, **93**; evolution of, 25–28, 30–31, 33, 35–36, 67, 74; family generations at, 9, 12, 27, **90**, 91–93, **92**, **93**; food influencers at, **43**, 43–45; Golden Cannoli at, **41**, 45, **45**, **78**, 79, **79**; Jenna's work and role at, 1, **35**, 91–92; learning curve in early days of, 11; lemon trees at, **24**, **31**, 33, 68, 82; L.J. working at, 92, **92**; menu revamp at, 33, 68, 74; music at, 31, 33, 37, 92–93; opening night after redesign, 67–68, **69–70**, 71, **71**, **72**, **73**, 73–74; outdoor dining at, 28, **32**, 33, **35**, 68, 77, 82; paintings at, 25, 37,

68; photo wall at, 55, **58**, 59–60, **61–62**, **63**, 63–65, **64**, **65**; politicians at, 9, 26, 27, 63, 74, **80**, 81–83, **82**; redesign and reopening of, 3, 12, 28, 30–31, 33, 35; Regis clothing line at, 60, **61**; Lawrence Scott's work at, **30**, 31, **31**, 33, 71, **72**, 74; Sylvester Stallone at, 26, **76**, 77, 79, **79**

Fresco by Scotto's Signature Meatballs, 161; Sunday Sauce with Meatballs, Sausages, and Pork Chops, **128**, 129

Fresco on the Go: opening of, 27; Rock and Hart performing at, 86–87, **87**; Sunset Lounge at, 33, **34**, 86, 92

Fritto Misto, **114**, 115

Frosé with Fresh Raspberries, 213

fusilli: Pesto Pasta with Potatoes, 137

Garganelli with Broccoli Rabe and Sausage, 148

garlic: Cauliflower and Roasted Garlic, 195; Garganelli with Broccoli Rabe and Sausage, 148; Garlic Sauce, 102, **103**; Pizzaiola Sauce, 170; Rigatoni with Short-Rib Ragù, 144–45; Roasted Garlic Mashed Potatoes, 174–75; tips for, 223

gin: Dress the Empress, 217

gnocchi, 130; Ricotta Gnocchi with Tomato Sauce, 146, **147**

goat cheese: Beet Salad with Toasted Pistachios, 126; Goat Cheese and Prosciutto Pinwheels, 106

Golden, Howard, 7

Golden Cannoli, **41**, 45, **45**, **78**, 79, **79**

Gorga, Joe and Melissa, **88**, 89

graham cracker crust: Chocolate Mascarpone Cream Pie, 208; Creamy Ricotta Cheesecake, 206, **207**

Grana Pedana cheese: Rosanna's Spaghetti alla Nerano, 136

grapefruit and grapefruit juice: Citrus Fregula Salad, 188–89; Paloma, The, 214

green beans. *See* haricots verts

Grilled Angus Sirloin Steak Pizzaiola with Simple Arugula Salad, **168**, 169–70

Grilled Branzino and Puttanesca Salsa Verde, 182, **183**

Grilled Pizza Margherita, 98–99

guanciale: Amatriciana, 149

Guest, Cornelia, 7–8, **8**

halibut, **120**, 121

haricots verts: Haricots Verts and Tomato, 196; Panzanella Salad, 187

Hart, Kevin, 75, 86–87, **87**

Harvey, Steve, 63, 64

Heller, Nicolas (New York Nico), 43–44

holiday sample menu, 218

Holiday Sour, 215

Homemade Pasta, 130

House-Made Ricotta with Lemon Zest Dip, **111**, 113

Instagram, 36, 39, 40, 41, 44, 45, 92. *See also* Scotto Sisters Schmoozing

Ischia island, Italy, 4–5

Italian sausage: Garganelli with Broccoli Rabe and Sausage, 148; Mama Scotto's Sausage and Rice Stuffing, 198; Sunday Sauce with Meatballs, Sausages, and Pork Chops, **128**, 129

Italy, 4–5, 33, 54–55, **55**

Jay-Z, **62**, 63

Jenna (Rosanna's daughter). *See* Ruggiero, Jenna

Johnson, Magic, **62**, 63

Jonas, Nick, 63

Julia (Elaina's daughter). *See* Faucetta, Julia

Kacmarcik, Benjamin, 33, 68, 74, 92

kale: Panzanella Salad, 187

Keller, Jaret, 74

Kotb, Hoda, 64

L'Acqua, Michaelangelo, 31, 33, 37

Lake Como, Italy, 54–55, **55**

lamb: Braised Lamb Shanks, 171; marinade, 162; Rack of Lamb, 162–63

Larry's Lemon Capellini Primavera, 74, **133**, 134–35

leeks: Mini Lentil Burgers, 107; Zuppa di Pesce, 118

lemon, 172–73, 179; Cannellini Bean Dip, 112; Chickpea alla Fresco Dip, 110, **111**; Citrus

Vinaigrette, 192; Frosé with Fresh Raspberries, 213; Holiday Sour, 215; House-Made Ricotta with Lemon Zest Dip, *111*, 113; Larry's Lemon Capellini Primavera, *133*, 134–35; Lemon-Caper Salsa Verde, 162–63; Lemon Gremolata, 135; Lemon Preserves, 135; Meyer, substitute for, 223

lemon grove, in Fresco by Scotto, *32*, 33, 42, 68, *68*, 82

lentils: Lentil Soup, 119; Mini Lentil Burgers, 107

lettuce: Beet Salad with Toasted Pistachios, 126; Fresco Burger, *158*, 159–60; Summer Salad, 122

Lil "Mo" Mozzarella, 43–44, *44*

lime juice, 214–17, **216**

Live with Kelly and Ryan, *73*, 74

L.J. (Rosanna's son). *See* Ruggiero, Louis, Jr.

lobster: how to cook, 152; Lobster Arancini, *184*, 185; Risotto with Lobster, Shrimp, and Calamari, 152–53; Seafood Stew or "Cioppino," **120**, 121

lobster roe, *184*, 185

lobster stock, 153; as crab stock alternative, 142

Los Angeles, California, 7–8, *8*

Mama Scotto (person). *See* Scotto, Marion

Mama Scotto (recipes): Mama Scotto's Sausage and Rice Stuffing, 198; Mom's Stuffed Mushrooms, 109

Manilow, Barry, 84–85, *85*

Maple Margarita, 215

margaritas, 215–16, **216**

marinades: chicken, 164; lamb, 162; steak, 172

marinara sauce: Amatriciana, 149; Garganelli with Broccoli Rabe and Sausage, 148; Pizzaiola Sauce, 170

Marinated Seafood Salad, 180

Martin, Jill, 47, 71

mascarpone: Chocolate Mascarpone Cream Pie, 208; Pumpkin Chocolate Tiramisu, 210; Scotto Polenta, 197

meatballs: Fresco by Scotto's Signature Meatballs, 161; Sunday Sauce with Meatballs, Sausages, and Pork Chops, 129

melon liqueur: Dress the Empress, 217; Melone Margarita, 216, **216**

menus, sample, 218–19

Meyer lemon substitute, 223

mezcal: Maple Margarita, 215

Miccio, Adina, 47

Mini Lentil Burgers, 107

mint: Shrimp with Watermelon and Tomato Salad, 124, *125*; Sun-Dried Tomato Pesto, 172–73

Mom's Stuffed Mushrooms, 109

mozzarella: Baked Ricotta Dip with Crostini, 102, **103**; Lobster Arancini, **184**, 185; Mama Scotto's Sausage and Rice Stuffing, 198; Mom's Stuffed Mushrooms, 109; Pizza Rustica, 116

mushrooms: Capellini with Mushroom Ragù, 132, **133**; Mom's Stuffed Mushrooms, 109; Penne Pasta Primavera, 131; Risotto with Wild Mushrooms, 154; Roasted Potatoes and Mushrooms, 157; tips for, 109, 132

mussels: Seafood Stew or "Cioppino," **120**, 121; Zuppa di Pesce, 118

Netanyahu, Benjamin, 75

New York City, 1–2, 25, **50**. *See also* Brooklyn family home; Fresco by Scotto

New York Nico (Nicolas Heller), 43–44

New York Post, **75**

New York Yankees, 59

octopus: Fritto Misto, **114**, 115; Marinated Seafood Salad, 180

O'Donnell, Rosie, 55, 64, **64**

olives: Pizzaiola Sauce, 170; Puttanesca Salsa Verde, 182, **183**

onions, red, 180, 189; Arugula and Red Onion Salad, 176; Zuppa di Pesce, 118

onions, red pearl: Haricots Verts and Tomato, 196

onions, Spanish: Amatriciana, 149; Braised Lamb Shanks, 171

oranges: Braised Short Ribs, 174–75; Citrus Fregula Salad, 188–89; Marinated Seafood Salad, 180; Shaved Fennel and Arugula Salad, 186

paccheri: Amatriciana, 149
Palminteri, Chazz, 43–44
Paloma, The, 214
pancetta: Fresco Burger, **158**, 159–60; Sunday Sauce with Meatballs, Sausages, and Pork Chops, **128**, 129
Panko. *See* bread crumbs
Pan-Seared Dover Sole with Sautéed Spinach, 181
Pan-Seared Salmon with Kale and Squash Panzanella Salad, 187
Pan-Seared Salmon with Shaved Fennel and Arugula Salad, 186
pantry list, 221
pappardelle, 130; Pappardelle with Pesto Genovese, 150–51
paprika, smoked, **114**, 115
Parmesan, 138; Baked Clams, 179; Baked Ricotta Dip with Crostini, 102, **103**; baking with topping of, 198; Capellini with Mushroom Ragù, 132, **133**; Eggplant and Zucchini Pie, 100–101; Fresco by Scotto's Signature Meatballs, 161; Goat Cheese and Prosciutto Pinwheels, 106; Grilled Angus Sirloin Steak, **168**, 169; House-Made Ricotta with Lemon Zest Dip, **111**, 113; Larry's Lemon Capellini Primavera, **133**, 134–35; Lobster Arancini, **184**, 185; Mama Scotto's Sausage and Rice Stuffing, 198; Parmesan-Crusted Mashed Potatoes, 193; Penne Pasta Primavera, 131; Pesto, 137; Pesto Genovese, 150–51; Prosciutto-Wrapped Asparagus with Parmesan Cheese, 108; Ricotta Gnocchi with Tomato Sauce, 146, **147**; Risotto with Wild Mushrooms, 154; Veal Milanese, 166–67, **167**
party sample menu, 219
pasta: dough, tips for, 130, 223; Homemade Pasta, 130; Pasta Bolognese, 138; Sunday Sauce with Meatballs, Sausages, and Pork Chops, **128**, 129. *See also specific types of pasta*
pâté à glacer: Chocolate Sauce, **202**, 202–3
peas: Tagliolini with Crab Ragù, **140**, 141–42
Pecorino Romano: Grilled Pizza Margherita, 98–99; Pesto, 137; Pizza Rustica, 116
Penne Pasta Primavera, 131
pesto: Baked Clams, 179; Pesto Genovese, 150–51; Pesto Pasta with Potatoes, 137; Sun-Dried Tomato Pesto, 172–73
Philbin, Regis, 60, **61**
pici, 130
pickles: Fresco Burger, **158**, 159–60; homemade, 160
pineapple juice: Dress the Empress, 217; La Resistenza, 217
pine nuts: Pesto, 137; Pesto Genovese, 150–51
pistachios: Beet Salad with Toasted Pistachios, 126
pizza: Grilled Pizza Margherita, 98–99; Pizza Rustica, 116
Pizzaiola Sauce, 170; Grilled Angus Sirloin Steak Pizzaiola, **168**, 169–70
polenta: Scotto Polenta, 197
politicians, 9, 26, 27, 63, 74, **80**, 81–83, **82**

pomegranate: Citrus Fregula Salad, 188–89; Pomegranate Tequila Cocktail, 212
Ponte Vecchio (restaurant), 19
porcini mushrooms, 154
pork chops: Sunday Sauce with Meatballs, Sausages, and Pork Chops, **128**, 129
potatoes: boiling, 221; Mashed Potatoes, 165; Parmesan-Crusted Mashed Potatoes, 193; Pesto Pasta with Potatoes, 137; Roasted Fingerling Potatoes, 194; Roasted Garlic Mashed Potatoes, 174–75; Roasted Potatoes and Mushrooms, 157
Prime Rib with Roasted Potatoes and Mushrooms, 156–57
prosciutto: Braised Short Ribs, 174; Pizza Rustica, 116; Prosciutto-Wrapped Asparagus with Parmesan Cheese, 108
Prosecco: Watermelon Bliss, 212
provolone: Fresco Burger, **158**, 159–60; Fresco by Scotto's Signature Meatballs, 161; Pizza Rustica, 116
Pumpkin Chocolate Tiramisu, 210

Quinoa Arugula Salad with Citrus Vinaigrette, 192
QVC partnership, xvi, 11–12, **46**, 47, **48**, 48–49

Rack of Lamb with Cannellini Bean Salad and Lemon-Caper Salsa Verde, 162–63
radishes: Shaved Fennel and Arugula Salad, 186; Summer Salad, 122–23

raspberries: Frosé with Fresh Raspberries, 213
Raspberry Vinaigrette, 123
Ravioli with Brown Butter Sage Sauce, 139
Real Housewives, 88, 89, **89**
Red Wine Vinaigrette, 123; Arugula Salad, 167, **167**, 173; Shrimp with Watermelon and Tomato Salad, 124, **125**; Simple Arugula Salad, 170
Resistenza, La, 217
ribs: Braised Short Ribs, 174–75; Rigatoni with Short-Rib Ragù, 144–45
rice: Lobster Arancini, **184**, 185; Mama Scotto's Sausage and Rice Stuffing, 198; Risotto with Lobster, Shrimp, and Calamari, 152–53; Risotto with Wild Mushrooms, 154
ricotta: Baked Ricotta Dip with Crostini, 102, **103**; Bomboloni, **202**, 202; Creamy Ricotta Cheesecake, 206, **207**; House-Made Ricotta with Lemon Zest Dip, **111**, 113; Pappardelle with Pesto Genovese, 150–51; Pizza Rustica, 116; Ricotta Fritters, 209; Ricotta Gnocchi with Tomato Sauce, 146, **147**
ricotta salata, 124, 176
rigatoni: Rigatoni with Short-Rib Ragù, 144–45; Sunday Sauce with Meatballs, Sausages, and Pork Chops, 129
Ripa, Kelly, 60, **70**, 71, 73, **73**, 74
risotto: Risotto with Lobster, Shrimp, and Calamari, 152–53; Risotto with Wild Mushrooms, 154
Roasted Fingerling Potatoes, 194

Roasted Garlic Mashed Potatoes, 174–75
Roasted Half Chicken with Mashed Potatoes, 164
Roasted Potatoes and Mushrooms, 156–57
Rock, Chris, 75, 86–87, **87**
Roker, Al, **52**, 64
Rosanna's Spaghetti alla Nerano, 136
rosé, 213
Rosie O'Donnell Show, 55, 64, **64**
Ruggiero, Jenna, 2, 3–4, **50**, **69**, **93**; with celebrities, **76**, **87**; editorial work for Scotto Sisters, 41, 92, 93; Fresco work and role of, 1, **35**, 91–92; Sylvester Stallone at Fresco and, **76**, 79; at Sunday Supper, **18**, 21
Ruggiero, Louis, 1, **2**, 3, **18**, **50**
Ruggiero, Louis, Jr. (L.J.), 1, **2**, 21, 54, 92, **92**, **93**

sage: Ravioli with Brown Butter Sage Sauce, 139
salmon: Pan-Seared Salmon, 186, **187**; Seafood Stew or "Cioppino," **120**, 121
salsa verde: Lemon-Caper Salsa Verde, 162–63; Puttanesca Salsa Verde, 182, **183**
sausage: Garganelli with Broccoli Rabe and Sausage, 148; Lentil Soup, 119; Mama Scotto's Sausage and Rice Stuffing, 198; soppressata, 116; Sunday Sauce with Meatballs, Sausages, and Pork Chops, **128**, 129
scallops: Seared Scallops, 188
Scott, Lawrence (Larry), **30**, 31, **31**, 33, 71, **72**, 74

Scotto, Andrew, **65**
Scotto, Anthony, Sr. (Dad), *xvii*, 10, **17**, **22**, **30**; Bill Clinton and, 80, 83; death of, 12–13, 23, 77; Fresco reopening photos of, **69**; Ischia as childhood home of, 4–5; at Lake Como, Italy, 54–55, **55**; in Los Angeles, 8, **8**; paintings commissioned by, 25, **27**, 68; QVC shows and, 11–12; role of, at Fresco, 9, 91; Sunday Supper and, 14, **18**, **19**, 20, 21, 23
Scotto, Anthony, Jr., 7, **17**, **26**, **52**; with celebrities, **62**, **80**; at *Rosie O'Donnell Show*, **64**; *Today Show* and, 54, **56**, 64
Scotto, Anthony, III, **65**
Scotto, Bianca, **65**
Scotto, Elaina, *ii*, *xviii*, **17**, **22**, **30**, **38**, **40**, **43**, **50**, **57**; birth of, 1; blended family of, **4**, 4; career in fashion, 4, 25; with celebrities, **9**, **26**, **60**, **62**, **64**, **76**, **80**, **87**, **88**, **89**; favorite things, 5; food influencers hosted by, 43–45, **44**, **45**; Fresco reopening photos of, **66**, **70**, **72**; QVC role of, **46**, **48**, 49; relationship with sister, 1, 2, 3, 5; Sunday Supper and, 14, **18**, 20; *Today Show* and, 51, **52**, 53, **56**
Scotto, Elaina, children of. *See* Faucetta, Danny; Faucetta, Julia
Scotto, Gabriella, **65**
Scotto, John, **17**, **57**; career of, 7–8; friendship with Sylvester Stallone, 7–8, **8**, 77; *Today Show* and, **52**, **56**
Scotto, Maria Elena, **65**
Scotto, Marion (Mom; Mama Scotto), 10, **17**,

30, *38*, *40*; with celebrities, **26**, **56**, **60**, **63**, **80**; childhood, 15, **16**; Hillary Clinton and, 11, **80**; Fresco management by, 11, 12, 91; Fresco opening and, 8–9; Fresco reopening photos of, **72**; importance of family, 7, 9; interpretation of suitcase painting, 37; at Lake Como, Italy, 54–55, **55**; and QVC partnership, 11; at *Rosie O'Donnell Show*, 64, **64**; Scotto Sisters Schmoozing and, 12, 28, 39, 42, **43**; and Dee Snider, 63, **63**; Sunday Supper and, 7, 15–16, **18**, 21, 23; *Today Show* and, 51, **52**, 53, **56**; volunteering work of, 7, 19

Scotto, Rosanna, ii, xviii, **17**, **22**, *30*, *38*, *40*, **43**, **50**, **57**; career as reporter, 1, 3, 28, 51, **52**, 53, **57**; with celebrities, **26**, **60**, **61**, **62**, **64**, **70**, **73**, **80**, **85**, **87**, **88**, **89**; Christmas Eve memory, 2; favorite things, 3; food influencers hosted by, 43–45, **44**, **45**; Fresco reopening photos of, **66**, **69**, **72**, **73**; as *Good Day New York* co-host, 57, 65; marriage and children, 1–2; relationship with sister, 1, **2**, 3, 5; Sunday Supper and, **14**, **18**, **20**, 21; *Today Show* and, 51, **52**, 53, **56**

Scotto, Rosanna, children of. *See* Ruggiero, Jenna; Ruggiero, Louis, Jr.

Scotto, Theresa, **65**

Scotto Polenta, 197

Scotto Sisters Schmoozing, **43**; creation and evolution of, xv–xvi, 39–45; followers of, 35–36, 39, 42; on Instagram, xvi, 12, 28, **29**, 41–42; Jenna as editor of, 41, 92; launch of, 28; Mama Scotto's role in, 12, 28, 39, 42

sea bass: Zuppa di Pesce, 118

seafood: Fritto Misto, **114**, 115; Risotto with Lobster, Shrimp, and Calamari, 152–53; Seafood Stew or "Cioppino," **120**, 121; tips about, 142, 152, 222; Zuppa di Pesce, 118. *See also specific seafood and fish*

seafood stock: Lobster Arancini, **184**, 185

Seared Scallops, Citrus Fregula Salad, and Cauliflower Puree, 188–89

serrano pepper, 160

shallots: Amatriciana, 149; Capellini with Mushroom Ragù, 132; Cauliflower Puree, 189; Fresco Burger, 159; Lobster Arancini, 185; Pappardelle with Pesto Genovese, 150; Pizzaiola Sauce, 170; Rigatoni with Short-Rib Ragù, 144; Risotto with Lobster, Shrimp, and Calamari, 152; steak marinade, 172; substitute for, 223; Summer Salad, 122

short ribs: Braised Short Ribs, 174–75; Rigatoni with Short-Rib Ragù, 144–45

shrimp: Fritto Misto, **114**, 115; Marinated Seafood Salad, 180; Risotto with Lobster, Shrimp, and Calamari, 152–53; Seafood Stew or "Cioppino," **120**, 121; Shrimp with Watermelon and Tomato Salad, 124, **125**; Zuppa di Pesce, 118

Shuter, Rob, 71, 84

Snider, Dee, 63, **63**

sole: Pan-Seared Dover Sole, 181; Tomato-and-Herb-Crusted Filet of Sole, 178

soppressata: Pizza Rustica, 116

spaghetti: Rosanna's Spaghetti alla Nerano, 136

spinach: Capellini with Mushroom Ragù, 132, **133**; Pesto Genovese, 150–51; Sautéed Spinach, 181

squash, summer. *See* yellow squash; zucchini

squash, winter: Panzanella Salad, 187

Stallone, Sylvester, 7–8, **8**, 26, 75, **76**, 77, 79, **79**

steak: Balsamic Skirt Steak, 172–73; Grilled Angus Sirloin Steak Pizzaiola with Simple Arugula Salad, **168**, 169–70; Prime Rib, 156–57

Steinbrenner, George, III, 59–60, **60**

Streisand, Barbra, 60, **61**, 75

Summer Salad with Raspberry Vinaigrette, 122–23

Sunday Sauce with Meatballs, Sausages, and Pork Chops, **128**, 129

Sunday Supper tradition, 7, **14**, 15–23, **18**, **19**, **20**

Sun-Dried Tomato Pesto, 172–73

Sussman, Bruce, 84–85, **85**

Tagliolini with Crab Ragù, **140**, 141–42

tahini: Cannellini Bean Dip, 112; Chickpea alla Fresco Dip, **110**, **111**

Tajin bitters, 217

television shows: *The Ellen DeGeneres Show*, 27, 55, 57, 64; *Live with Kelly and Ryan*, 73, 74; *Rosie O'Donnell Show*, 55, 64, **64**; *Today Show*, 27, 51, **52**, 53, **56**, 59, 64

tequila, 3; Melone Margarita, 216, **216**; The Paloma, 214; Pomegranate Tequila Cocktail, 212; La Resistenza, 217. *See also* mezcal

Today Show, 27, 51, **52**, 53, 59, 64, **64**

tomatoes: Arugula and Red Onion Salad, 176; Arugula Salad, 167, **167**, 173; Citrus Fregula Salad, 188–89; Elaina's Tomato Bruschetta, **104**, 105; Fresco Burger, **158**, 159–60; Haricots Verts and Tomato, 196; peeling, 223; Penne Pasta Primavera, 131; Rigatoni with Short-Rib Ragù, 144–45; Shrimp with Watermelon and Tomato Salad, 124, **125**; Tomato-and-Herb-Crusted Filet of Sole, 178; Zuppa di Pesce, 118

tomatoes, canned: Lentil Soup, 119; Seafood Stew or "Cioppino," **120**, 121; Sunday Sauce with Meatballs, Sausages, and Pork Chops, **128**, 129; Tagliolini with Crab Ragù, **140**, 141–42; Tomato Sauce, 143

tomatoes, sun-dried: Sun-Dried Tomato Pesto, 172–73

tomato juice: Seafood Stew or "Cioppino," **120**, 121

tomato paste: Braised Lamb Shanks, 171; crab stock, 142; Lobster Arancini, **184**, 185; lobster stock, 153

tomato puree: Braised Short Ribs, 174–75

tomato sauce: Eggplant and Zucchini Pie, 100–101; Grilled Pizza Margherita, 98–99; Haricots Verts and Tomato, 196; Pasta Bolognese, 138; recipe, 143; Ricotta Gnocchi with Tomato Sauce, 146, **147**; Risotto with Lobster, Shrimp, and Calamari, 152–53

triple sec: Maple Margarita, 215; Melone Margarita, 216, **216**

Trump, Donald, 63

Trump, Ivana, **62**, 63

utensils, 220, 222

vanilla puree: Bomboloni, 202, **202**

veal: Mama Scotto's Sausage and Rice Stuffing, 198; Veal Milanese, 166–67, **167**

veal stock: Rigatoni with Short-Rib Ragù, 144–45

vinegar and vinaigrettes. *See* balsamic vinegar and glaze; champagne vinegar; Citrus Vinaigrette; Raspberry Vinaigrette; Red Wine Vinaigrette

vodka: Watermelon Bliss, 212

watermelon: Shrimp with Watermelon and Tomato Salad, 124, **125**; Watermelon Bliss, 212

whitefish puree: Cod Puree Dip, 110, **111**

Williams, Wendy, **70**, 71

wine, red, 19; Braised Lamb Shanks, 171; Braised Short Ribs, 174–75; Pizzaiola Sauce, 170; Rigatoni with Short-Rib Ragù, 144–45; Seafood Stew or "Cioppino," **120**, 121; Sunday Sauce with Meatballs, Sausages, and Pork Chops, **128**, 129

wine, rosé: Frosé with Fresh Raspberries, 213

wine, white: Amatriciana, 149; Capellini with Mushroom Ragù, 132, **133**; crab stock, 142; Garganelli with Broccoli Rabe and Sausage, 148; Larry's Lemon Capellini Primavera, **133**, 134–35; Lobster Arancini, **184**, 185; Marinated Seafood Salad, 180; Pan-Seared Dover Sole, 181; Pappardelle with Pesto Genovese, 150–51; Pasta Bolognese, 138; Risotto with Lobster, Shrimp, and Calamari, 152–53; Zuppa di Pesce, 118

yellow squash: Larry's Lemon Capellini Primavera, **133**, 134–35; Rosanna's Spaghetti alla Nerano, 136; Summer Salad, 122–23

Yormark family (Brett, Drake, and Madison), 4, **4**

zucchini: Eggplant and Zucchini Pie, 100–101; Fritto Misto, **114**, 115; Larry's Lemon Capellini Primavera, **133**, 134–35; Penne Pasta Primavera, 131; Rosanna's Spaghetti alla Nerano, 136

Zuppa di Pesce, 118

Sharing Our Family Traditions for over 30 Years.

Join us for a memorable lunch or dinner.

34 East 52nd Street
New York, NY

Catering and Special Events

40 East 52nd Street
New York, NY

www.frescobyscotto.com